EXPLORING CALIFORNIA BYWAYS · II

In and around Los Angeles

Trips for a day or a weekend

BY RUSS LEADABRAND

THE WARD RITCHIE PRESS · LOS ANGELES

Based on a series of articles by Russ Leadabrand.
Originally published in Westways,
the official Publication of the
Automobile Club of Southern California.
Revised by Russ Leadabrand, 1968

First Printing, October 1968
Second Printing, April 1969

TO MICHAEL LEADABRAND

who had the courage to go
when the time was right;
and the sensitivity to
look back and wave . . .

COVER PHOTO: *View of Fort Tejon State Park.*
BACK COVER: *View of Queen Anne's Cottage at*
State and County Arboretum in Arcadia.
Photo by the author.

PREFACE

Russ Leadabrand's series of monthly articles on trips into California's backcountry have been appearing in *Westways* for nine years now. That's a long time for any series.

I have often wondered when the popularity of these articles would wane, for as times change so do people's tastes and preferences for passing their leisure time—whether in travel or reading. Yet that popularity has not flagged.

There were times when Russ and I feared (Russ less so than I, to be sure) that we might soon exhaust the amount of roads, lore and mere geography that are the substance of these quiet adventures. As yet we have not, and that fact has taught me that southern California is an even larger and more richly endowed region than I had ever imagined. It has also taught me that there is much of California which remains unspoiled or only slightly violated—despite the real and devastating assaults by "progress" on the land reported almost daily by the media.

Still, all this does not account for the reader reception given the magazine articles and the first collection of byway stories printed by the Ward Ritchie Press last year. For that you must speculate about the nature of the readers themselves.

Perhaps Marshall McLuhan and the apostles of the "now generation" have missed the point. Or bent it. Perhaps "all-at-onceness" and "post linearity" are descriptive of a time in life rather than the essence of a new generation.

It would seem that most people, sooner or later, feel at least an occasional urge to seek out the past, to know who was here before and what they left behind. A sense of continuity is balm to many ills.

And sooner or later people feel the need to return to nature—to trees and streams and rocks—for nourishment and a sense of place. After all, man has lived longer in the company of forests and deserts and mountains than he has lived with television sets or computers.

Nature, of course, does not need anyone to speak for it, though interpreters it deserves, and Russ Leadabrand has proven himself a most sensitive one with his lucid and shyly lyric prose style. And few, if any, know as much about the land and lore of rustic southern California as does Russ.

The trips for this book have been selected with an immediacy to the Los Angeles area in mind. Though a few actually traverse what might be considered urban centers, the descriptive tenor is essentially nostalgic and the pastimes recommended, of a peaceful sort. The majority of trips, however, will take you off the beaten track into more bucolic—even rugged—surroundings. The local-history-conscious, the mining buff, the amateur naturalist and geologist, the ghost-town lover, the jeep-road adventurer, or the family simply fond of weekend drives will find much here to please them.

LARRY L. MEYER

July 1968
Los Angeles

vi

CONTENTS

INTRODUCTION

The success of the first book collection of *Let's Explore a Byway* articles has resulted in this second offering. This time there are fifteen articles. This time they are all fairly close in to the Los Angeles area. Some stray off into Kern, San Bernardino, Orange Counties, but essentially they are all trips that could be driven in a day or weekend from the Los Angeles region.

At the publication of this book the *Byway* series has gone into a ninth year in Westways. It has seen two editors during its run. Miss Patrice Manahan retired in 1967 and her able and talented assistant editor, Larry Meyer, has now assumed command of the publication. It has been a joy to work with both of these fine people.

I am forever amazed at the country my byway exploring takes me to. For a while I was busy crossing off a map the middle-sized and smaller roads that I had driven. In recent years I have taken the byway explorers on a number of even lesser roads. It has all been good adventure and the comments from readers have encouraged me to try new corners of the state. In 1968 byway explorations took me as far north as the California-Oregon border, and south into Mexico.

And still the maps offer new areas to explore, spots where I have never been. Little roads that beckon, smaller roads that invite.

Perhaps in time, all of California could be thus explored. But I doubt it. The state is too large.

As long as there is a demand, we will continue to explore the byways and to report on them.

Those who have helped get this second *Byway* book together have been many. Larry Meyer and Bill Newbro and the staff at

Westways were invaluable. At The Ward Ritchie Press I've had help from Dick Lewis, Bob Weinstein and Cas Duchow.

My favorite traveling companion, Barbara Leadabrand, has made most of the outings pleasant. We have had some delightful picnic lunches along the way.

My hope is that you enjoy exploring these byways as much as we did. We had fun.

I ACROSS THE TOP OF THE SAN GABRIEL MOUNTAINS

Fun to explore—any time but during heavy snows
Length of exploration—can be driven in a day

IT WASN'T LONG AGO, easily within the memory of many southern Californians, when there were no roads across the roof of the San Gabriel Mountains of Los Angeles County.

Today the roads are many and they span the mountains in such a way that it is possible to chart a great snake-shaped route across the range. This is the byway we will explore, and the roads vary from the busy Angeles Forest and Angeles Crest Highways to the seldom-used Aliso Canyon and Glendora Ridge roads.

Toward the end of the last century the value of the San Gabriel Mountains was recognized. Here were not only recreation lands, game and timber, but most important, the watershed that nurtured the valleys below. In 1892 the San Gabriel Timberland Reserve was created. Today most of these mountains are under the aegis of the Angeles National Forest.

The road up the Little Tujunga starts at Foothill Boulevard within sight of Hansen Dam just east of San Fernando. While this road along the west end of the mountains dates back more than thirty years, there are ranches that are at least three decades older.

In time a paved road went through, following the boulder-strewn bottom of the Little T., zigzagging up the side of the high ridge that culminates with Mendenhall Peak and finally reaching Dillon Divide.

From this point on north the chaparral-grown canyon is part of the Pacoima Canyon drainage. In the stream bottom stands alders

*The East Fork of the San Gabriel River frequently runs full
enough to invite attentions of serious and enthused anglers*

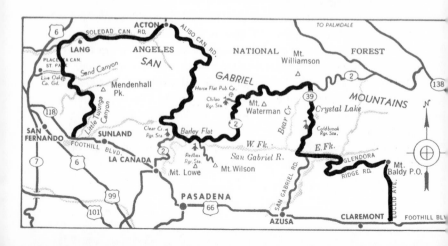

and sycamores, and there's a private trout farm with picnic facilities.

Then the errant road climbs again, reaching this time for the ridge that separates the Pacoima from Sand Canyon.

On the bank of the stream bed is the Live Oak Forest Service campground, certainly not the greenest site in the Angeles National Forest, but always a popular one.

A mile or so beyond Live Oak, and in cattle and farming country now, a paved road bends away to the west and runs into Placerita Canyon State and County Park and to the historic landmark oak under which gold was first discovered in California in 1842.

Straight ahead the Sand Canyon road runs through farmland and then debouches into the Santa Clara River, crossing the Southern Pacific Railroad tracks near the historic golden spike community of Lang.

We turn to the east here, follow the Soledad Canyon Road, pass under the new Antelope Valley Freeway which is now complete deep into the Antelope Valley, run along the northern edge of Angeles Forest and through the railroad communities of Ravenna and Acton.

Just east of Acton a good paved byway signed Aliso Canyon Road runs south toward the burned and barren hills, the northern face of the San Gabriels. But there are many springs hidden along this seared flank. One such lush green spot is Magnetic Springs, bearing another one of those curious place names. (Why is Magic Mountain so named?)

The Aliso Canyon Road passes bee ranches and orchards, swings in a slow arc to connect with the Angeles Forest Highway just south of Kentucky Springs.

From here to the junction with the Angeles Crest Highway at Clear Creek the byway explorer will be traveling the most heavily used route connecting the San Gabriel Valley area with the Antelope Valley. The road climbs swiftly on its way south to the Mill Creek Summit (Tie Summit), then drops down into the drainage of Mill Creek.

Passing through a tunnel the Forest Highway suddenly overlooks The Narrows of the Big Tujunga, an impressive chasm. On the bridge that crosses the cleft there is a rustic stone lookout station. Then, up along the east rim of the Big Tujunga, the Forest Highway hugs the cliff all the way in to Clear Creek.

At Clear Creek junction we turn east, following the popular Angeles Crest Highway up the Upper Arroyo Seco to Red Box.

East of Red Box a great valley yawns and beckons. This is the wooded West Fork of the San Gabriel River.

There is a friendly dirt road from Red Box down into the West Fork. It passes Camp Hi-Hill—old Opid's Camp—the Long Beach City Schools' exciting program of outdoor education participated in by each sixth-grade class from that beach community. There are isolated islands of private land along the canyon, holdovers from the early days when the traffic here was up from the valley via the old Sturtevant Trail.

The West Fork dirt road is a good one, but frequently it is only wide enough for one-way traffic. In the canyon bottom is the pleasant campground of Valley Forge.

Six miles from Red Box is the historic West Fork station, the oldest structure on the Angeles National Forest, the oldest ranger station in California. The original station here was built between 1896 and 1900 and was occupied variously until the 1930's. It is still utilized as a storehouse and is slated for restoration into a small forest museum.

The most famous site in the entire San Gabriel Mountains can be reached via a good paved road from Red Box. This site, of course, is Mount Wilson, made famous by the Carnegie Institution

6

of Washington's installations which have stood on the crest since 1904.

The five-mile, high-gear drive from Red Box up to the top of the 5,710-foot peak gives little hint of the work involved in getting the parts of the famous 100-inch Hooker telescope—many of them large and cumbersome, others delicate—up the old Mount Wilson Toll Road on the seaward side of the mountains.

Much of this almost-forgotten road was shaped to accommodate the hauling of the telescope parts. It still stands today, narrow, steep, cliff-hanging in places, frequently spooky and now closed to vehicular traffic.

By comparison the road up from Red Box has almost no spooky spots. At the Eaton Canyon Saddle the fire road and trail branch off and lead down to Mount Lowe. These are within the summer fire season closures. Such closures have been adopted by the Forest Service both as a public safety measure and a fire prevention precaution.

Near the summit the antennas of southern California's seven television stations stand like a glittering metallic forest. Beyond is the gate where you enter Mount Wilson Skyline Park, a new development created from the old Mount Wilson resort by Metromedia. Here you'll find a parking area, a pavilion where snacks and souvenirs are sold. There are picnic tables and in time the area will be further developed with a lake and many trails. The old Mount Wilson Hotel is gone, erased are the sites of old Child's Camp and Strain's Camp, once headquarters for hikers in the San Gabriel Mountains.

There is a short hike to the Carnegie Institution's astronomical museum and the big 100-inch telescope. You can look at the monster sky searcher through a view port but not through the telescope itself.

The Angeles Crest Highway points eastward from Red Box and

7

Lodgepole pines, rarely seen on southern California mountains,
stand straight and crowded along the trail
to Mount Baden-Powell

on clear days, from certain bright points along this route, the great two-mile-high uplifts of Waterman and Twin Peaks can be seen.

This is mountain driving at its simplest. The road here is almost without change in altitude. There are numerous turnouts from which views down into the deep West Fork are unobstructed.

Here, on the left, is the paved turnoff back to the old Nike site at Barley Flats; it is now a county construction camp. Also on the left is the unpaved road that winds down into the Big Tujunga drainage. This interesting byway is within the fire closure by summer, but put it on your list for a fascinating fair weather fall drive.

Charleton Flat is for day use only. Chilao is for camping and caters to both tent campers and trailers. (Not far away, by a good dirt road, is Horse Flats, another big camping area. Near here, too, is the Bandito camp, which caters to organizations and horsemen.)

In the old days Charlton Flat was known as Pine Flat and the original trail to the area was laid out by Jim Akin and George Islip. Later a shorter course into Pine Flat was charted by Louie Newcomb and this became the well-known Shortcut Canyon Trail.

Rangers on the site lived in tents until 1902 and in that year the first cabin was built, shaded handsomely by pines and spruce. In 1931, and for the following five years, the city of Pasadena managed the Flat under a special use permit and developed the recreational facilities here. The subsequent name, Charlton Flat, pays honor to R. H. Charlton, one of the early supervisors of the Angeles National Forest.

Just beyond Chilao stands the Newcomb Ranch Store near which Louie Newcomb built the first cabin on his patented claim back in 1890. Then the Angeles Crest Highway settles down to the more serious business of gaining altitude, reaching for 6,500-foot Cloudburst Summit on the flank of Mount Waterman.

Here, on the slopes of Waterman and Kratka Ridge, are some of the finest cedar, fir and pine in the Forest. Out beyond Cedar

Spring—for years the end-of-track for the inmate-constructed mountain highway—the byway reaches and pierces the great crumbly bluffs of Mount Williamson, and finally runs on to Islip Saddle.

To the south lies the giant trough of Bear Creek, within the San Gabriel Wilderness. To the west loom the stony battlements of Twin Peaks.

There is a road that flanks Bear Canyon. Called the Crystal Lake Road, it winds around the west face of fractured Mount Islip, curves under Crystal Lake and becomes an extension of State Highway 39, the San Gabriel Canyon Road.

To the east looms Mount South Hawkins with its fragile lookout tower perched aloft. The road to the tower is closed to vehicles, but it is a good hike from the Crystal Lake campground.

Alders, willows and sycamores put in an appearance as Highway 39 loses altitude. Coldbrook Forest Service camp is reached, we pass the opening to the opposite end of the West Fork from the one we explored out of Red Box, and then we come to Rincon. Beyond this point the terrain flattens and we reach the bridge that crosses the main riverbed into the East Fork of the San Gabriel River.

The San Gabriel River drainage, the main watershed of the entire mountain country, covers more than 375 square miles.

Along the East Fork of the San Gabriel River, as early as 1855, placer gold mining took place. For a while, between 1859 and 1862, the rockers and long toms were busy. The small mining camp of Eldoradoville sprang up in the bottom of the East Fork, and on January 18, 1862, was completely washed away by a cloudburst.

The county road once reached beyond Cattle Canyon and Camp Bonita and almost to The Narrows, but the flood of 1938 eliminated this highway.

10

From the end of the road along the canyon bottom a byway climbs stiffly up out of the East Fork. On the top of the ridge this byway joins the Glendora Ridge Road—an extension of the Glendora Mountain Road—a twisted, infrequently driven mountain thoroughfare that connects the Dalton Canyon country with San Antonio Canyon.

Drive northeast on this paved road. Look down into the basin on the right into the blackened ruin that was once the Forest Service San Dimas Experimental Station.

To the north rears the scarred massif of San Antonio Peak— Mount Baldy—at 10,059 feet, the highest mountain in the range.

The Glendora Ridge Road drops down into San Antonio Canyon near Mount Baldy Village. From here it is an easy drive to the parking area at the foot of Baldy and the year-around-operating chair lift. A return to the San Gabriel Valley can be made via the San Antonio Canyon road which returns to Foothill Boulevard by way of Euclid Avenue into Upland or Mills Avenue into Claremont.

It has been said that because of frequent earthquakes the San Gabriel Mountains are so shattered that they defy accurate geological classification. The San Andreas fault hugs the northern side of the range. Rainfall has been fickle and cruel. Once twenty-six inches fell in twenty-four hours in an area off the West Fork. There have been prolonged droughts. Fire has wrecked some of the proud timber stands and has damaged the watershed.

Thus beset by nature, whipped by scorching Santa Ana winds, its delicate biota menaced by air pollution, the San Gabriel Mountains still present a rugged charm. In a remote corner against lofty Mount Baden-Powell there are some weather-tortured limber pines that may rival the bristlecones of Inyo National Forest in age. Brown bear and bighorn sheep survive. Native trout are still being hooked in the Iron Fork country up the East Fork of the San

Gabriel River. There are lakes, and tall, aromatic russet-barked cedars, and icy springs.

The byway we have charted across the mountains barely stirs up the duff under a single tree of the forest in Los Angeles's back yard. Still it will introduce you to the many faces of the range, and chances are you'll come back to explore again.

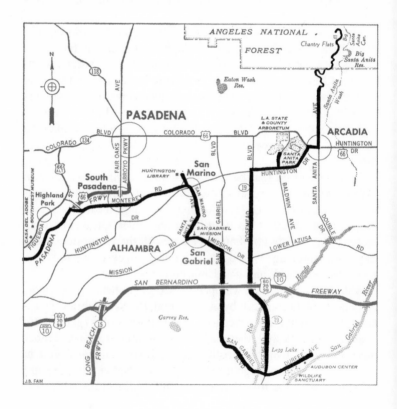

II THROUGH THE SAN GABRIEL VALLEY

Fun to explore—any time of the year
Length of exploration—can be seen in a day
Better for two days trip or weekend

THERE WAS A TIME when the major tourist attractions of southern California were grouped inland of Los Angeles in a corner of country you could roughly call the west San Gabriel Valley.

In their own way and time as famous as Disneyland is now were the Mt. Lowe Railway, the Cawston Ostrich Farm, Gay's Lion Farm and Busch's Gardens.

All are gone now. The determined hiker can find traces of the incredible old Mt. Lowe line in the purple-green chaparral of the San Gabriel Mountains. Cawston's Ostrich Farm in South Pasadena and Gay's Lion Farm in El Monte are lost without a trace. Busch's Gardens in Pasadena has left a few hints behind: a street name and some crumbling masonry.

Yet the gentle death of these landmarks in no way signaled the end of scenic attractions in the San Gabriel Valley. Other sites, less spectacular perhaps, have taken the place of the ostrichs and lions and mountain railroad.

Southern Californians can explore this handful of places in a day, or a weekend, or, if they have a mind, in a procession of weekends. For in addition to history—one of California's proud commodities often overlooked when put on display beside her fairer sister, climate—there are other values here to please the byway explorer: attractive gardens, sports, the subtle outdoor attractions of nature.

13

At the Southwest Museum in Highland Park there is a display devoted to talking stones. These cases are given over to the development of lithic tools—stone implements—by the aboriginal inhabitants of the western United States.

In the days before man knew the convenient cutting edge of metal, he used stone. With stone—first stream cobbles, then more workable materials such as flint, obsidian and chert—early man built first axes, hide flensers, knives, spear and throwing stick points, finally arrowheads. Some of these reflect an incredible skill with a stubborn material, a skill that Indians of today neither know nor remember. Few men in the world today can fashion even a passable Folsom point, true to its original design. That there were always craftsmen in the land becomes immediately apparent when one heeds the story these stone implements tell.

The Southwest Museum, a private, non-tax supported institution, is open to the public from 1:00 to 5:00 p.m. daily except Monday without charge. In it is one of the finest collections of Indian art and artifacts in the Southwest.

Perched on a commanding headland overlooking the Arroyo Seco called Museum Hill, the towered structure was the creation of Charles F. Lummis. It was Lummis' organization, the Southwest Society, that attracted the interested patrons and gathered sufficient cash to build the museum. The incorporation took place in 1907, the ground breaking waited until 1912. Principal donors in the beginning were Henry O'Melveny and Carrie M. Jones. Doors of the institution opened to the public "without fanfare or ceremony," according to historian W. W. Robinson, on August 3, 1914.

From 1932 until 1955 Dr. Frederick W. Hodge, noted American archaeologist-anthropologist, served as director of the Museum. He was succeeded in 1955 by the able Carl S. Dentzel.

There are two entrances to the Museum. From the lower level a

14

The Southwest Museum

tunnel, studded with many fascinating dioramas, leads to the museum elevator. A paved road leads up the hill behind the Museum where there is more adequate parking for visitors.

Included in the permanent displays are the art and artifacts of the Northwest Coast Hall, the Caroline Boeing Poole Basketry Hall, the Hinchman Hall of Southwestern Ethnology, the California Hall, the Plains Indian Hall.

The display of ancient stone tools and weapons is part of the Charles F. Lummis Hall of Prehistory.

There is a most excellent library at the Museum, used constantly by students of the Southwest who are attracted by the vast storehouse of books, serials and manuscripts, as well as by the cordial and stimulating atmosphere of a working museum.

It is easy to see the white tower of the Southwest Museum from El Alisal, the home of museum founder Charles F. Lummis. Situated just off the Pasadena Freeway on Avenue 43, in Highland Park, the Lummis Home today is a state historical landmark. Preserved by the state of California, it is maintained by the Los Angeles Department of Recreation and Parks aided by the Southwest Museum and the Charles F. Lummis Memorial Association.

Open daily except Saturday from 1:00 to 4:00 p.m., El Alisal was built under the shade of a vast sycamore tree about 1895. Lummis constructed his house largely of cobblestones from the nearby streambed of the Arroyo Seco.

Lummis was a man of many hats, a latter-day pioneer worthy of more attention than he receives. In addition to founding the Southwest Museum, he campaigned successfully to preserve and restore certain of southern California's crumbling missions. He was an author, a newsman, a librarian, a collector, a fighter for the rights of the American Indian. El Alisal, in its day, was the meeting place of the famous from the world of arts, letters and sciences, who came to meet this uncommon man.

Mention should also be made here of a Southwest Museum adjunct, Casa de Adobe, located just below the Museum at 4605 North Figueroa Street. This typical Spanish period home, with gardens and patio, is open to the public only on Wednesdays, Saturdays and Sundays from 2:00 to 5:00 p.m. Entrance to the Casa can best be made from Figueroa Street, not from the Museum parking area.

From the Lummis Home take the Pasadena Freeway east to the Fair Oaks Avenue off-ramp in South Pasadena. Follow Fair Oaks Avenue south to Monterey Road. Drive east on this thoroughfare through South Pasadena and San Marino then to Oxford Road and here turn left, north to the entrance to the Huntington Library.

The Henry E. Huntington Library and Art Gallery is internationally famed. A neglected companion, by comparison, is the outstanding botanical gardens which are less well known.

From the parking area of the library, off Oxford Road, the path to the Cactus Garden area lies to the south, gained by passing through the main pedestrian entrance and then curving around to the left and through the palm garden.

Here are ten acres devoted to a desert plant garden. The saguaro, the agave, the cholla, the ocotillo, the cirio are among the more common varieties. And, as would be expected here, there are many exotics. Some of the cacti may be in bloom just now. If so, the color photographer will enjoy capturing on film the delicate hues of cactus flowers. Incidentally, tripods are not allowed within the library grounds.

Opposite the Cactus Garden is the recently refurbished lily pond area. Tiny waterfalls and pools have been imaginatively created here in a section of the Huntington gardens first laid out sixty-two years ago.

Returning to the entrance area via the same path, the explorer now moves west along the front of the Library building through plantings of camellias and azaleas to the North Vista, a handsome, broad avenue of lawn bordered by more than thirty stone figures. The fountain at the focus of the North Vista is of Seventeenth Century Italian design.

Beyond the North Vista lies the Shakespeare Garden, planted with varieties mentioned by William Shakespeare in his many writings.

West, through the rose pergola, which looks out past the Rose Garden, lies the Japanese Garden, the high point of any trip to the Huntington grounds. This spot was Huntington's personal favorite, and here stands the bright red Moon Bridge arched gracefully over pond and plantings, and the Japanese tea house.

Flanking the handsome Oriental setting are the banks of camellias that have attracted annual comment. There are more than 1000 varieties of camellias in the five-acre plot alongside this hillside, with new types of plants going on display each season.

From here it is possible to return to the starting point of the walking tour via oak- or deodar-lined avenues. Some visitors may wish to explore the library and art gallery at greater leisure.

From the Huntington follow Oxford Drive south to Huntington Drive, west then to Cambridge Road, where we can cross the dividing section of the broad Huntington Drive, and turn back to the east. At San Marino Avenue we turn south, and when this road comes to a Y we bear right on Santa Anita Street, across Las Tunas Boulevard, to the San Gabriel Mission.

Neither the most attractive, nor the least, of California's restored missions, Mission San Gabriel Arcángel does possess a handsome chapel, a formal garden cum cemetery, and certain archaeological features of interest.

A venerable grape vine covers an arbored walk along the east side of the mission building. Here is a small museum in rooms once

18

*The outside stairway at the Mission San Gabriel Arcángel
which was founded by the Franciscan fathers
on September 8, 1771*

used by the padres as living quarters, with the usual collection of mission art, old books, vestments.

San Gabriel Arcángel was one of the more important in the chain of twenty-one Franciscan missions in the strange world of Alta California. Close to the pueblo of Los Angeles and beside a major east-west trail, it was founded September 8, 1771, by Frs. Pedro Benito Cambon and Angel Fernandez de la Somera, under orders of Fr. Serra. Frs. Cambon and Somera are buried under the floor of the mission sanctuary along with six others of the faithful.

After secularization Franciscan fathers stayed on in dwindling numbers as late as 1852. Then the last of the Franciscans moved to Santa Barbara and evidence indicates that San Gabriel Arcángel stood deserted for seven long years.

In 1859 President Buchanan signed the patent that gave the mission back to the Catholic Church. San Gabriel served as a parish church then until 1908 when the mission was entrusted to the Sons of the Immaculate Heart of Mary, popularly known as the Clarentian Fathers.

Today the mission is open daily from 9 a.m. to 6 p.m. Masses are conducted on weekdays and on Sundays. Entrance to the mission chapel, grounds and museum for visitors is through the mission gift shop.

Along the north bank of the San Gabriel River just upstream from the Whittier Narrows Dam lies the 125-acre Audubon Center of Southern California, a preserve dedicated to promote the understanding of man's relationship with the natural world.

Operated by the National Audubon Society and open to the public without charge, the Center provides a museum and a series of river bottom trails that probe into a sprawling and fascinating plant and wildlife sanctuary.

Here the visitor can get as intimate with nature as he wishes. He can watch the ragged flight of crows, he can ponder the web building of a striped spider, or he can study the tiny track of a beetle in the soft dirt of a trail.

Birds are frequent visitors here—as are bird watchers. At least one instructor-naturalist is on hand early each day to walk the trails looking for good examples of opossum, skunk or rabbit tracks to protect and mark for later visitors.

School and youth groups make regular pilgrimages to the sanctuary and a trained guide takes them along one of the marked trails, explaining conservation and the balance of nature and the patient interrelated rhythm of plants and animals in an undisturbed world.

The preserve was born in 1939 as the San Gabriel River Sanctuary, has undergone size alterations and legal restrictions until today the 125 acres are leased from the government. In 1955 a fire charred forty-five acres of the preserve, but this, left to nature to rebuild, has slowly come back and now offers ground cover of many different local and induced types.

The sanctuary is located at 1000 Durfee Avenue in El Monte and can be reached from the San Gabriel Mission by traveling from the historic site south on Mission Road to San Gabriel Boulevard, then continuing south on San Gabriel Boulevard on its curve down and across Rosemead Boulevard. Just as it crosses Rosemead Boulevard, San Gabriel Boulevard becomes Durfee Avenue. The Audubon Center is located a short distance to the east.

The Center is open daily except Sunday and legal holidays from 9:00 a.m. to 5:00 p.m. There is a staff of trained naturalists on hand. Those wishing to make arrangements for tours by organizational groups of eight or more should telephone 444-1872 for an appointment. Picnicking, pets and recreational games are not allowed in the sanctuary. But the fascination of following the five miles of nature trails noting the insignificant such as the bright flash of the cardinal, or an insect gall, or a spider's egg sac, or a

*Fed by underground springs is this palm-fringed lagoon at the
Arboretum in Arcadia. Many jungle films have been
made at this San Gabriel Valley site*

22

furtive rabbit in the weed and ubiquitous wild grape tangles, can be quietly satisfying.

On Lake Aquatecas migratory water fowl make their home at the six-year-old lake. Many coot, mallards and an occasional heron have stopped off here briefly.

From the Audubon Center of Southern California the best route to follow to the Los Angeles State and County Arboretum in Arcadia is: return to Rosemead Boulevard, drive north to Huntington Drive, east then on Huntington to Baldwin Avenue in Arcadia. North on Baldwin Avenue is the parking area for the Arboretum. (Just to the east is Santa Anita Park, southern California's beautiful race track.)

There is something for everyone at the Arboretum.

For the history buff there is the restored Queen Anne Cottage of Lucky Baldwin, and the Hugo Reid adobe. Indians freely roamed the site in pre-mission days, and they left their mark here.

For the gardener—professional, amateur or armchair—there is an abundance: orchids, herbs, ornamentals, exotic and native plants.

For the nature student, the Arboretum is a bird sanctuary.

For the youngster, there is the Lasca Lagoon and the fringe jungle country with suitable tangled trails. Scores of motion pictures have been made here, most notably many of the Tarzan films.

For the artist, here is landscape of a surprising variety, and almost every day sees representatives of this fraternity on hand, usually near the lagoon or Queen Anne Cottage.

Peacocks rule the Arboretum with a casual air, sometimes haughtily blocking foot traffic. Some say they date back to the Baldwin era.

There are regularly scheduled jeep train trips around the 127-acre preserve, and a driver-guide points out the features of interest during the circuit of the grounds. Naturalists are also on hand.

Actually the Arboretum plays a more important role than catering to visitors. It is a horticultural test center where plants used to beautify southern California gardens, parks and parkways are studied. It is a school for gardeners, garden superintendents, propagators and other skilled personnel required by commercial and private nurseries and gardens. It is a research center, working in collaboration with educational institutions and various government departments of agriculture. Here is a catalog of all plants cultivated in southern California, where specimens can be readily identified. Here is a horticulture library and herbarium. Technical papers are published from the Arboretum.

The Queen Anne Cottage was built by Lucky Baldwin around 1881. Within the last decade it has been handsomely restored, repainted, brought back to its Victorian charm by the Historical Committee of the California Arboretum Foundation, Inc. It is a museum today. A peek through the various windows of the cottage provides a glimpse into a less hectice way of life. The Hugo Reid Adobe, recently excavated and restored, has similarly been turned into a window-view museum. The adobe grounds include reproductions of both the Spanish and Indian period structures.

There is no admission charge to the Los Angeles State and County Arboretum. It is open from 9:00 a.m. to 5:30 p.m. seven days of the week. The jeep train runs from 10:30 a.m. to 4:00 p.m. on each half hour.

From Baldwin Avenue and Colorado Boulevard our byway runs east to Santa Anita Avenue—Double Drive—in Arcadia, turns north here and runs back into the San Gabriel Mountains.

At the end of this mountain road is Chantry Flats, one of the Angeles National Forest's most heavily used picnic grounds, and jumping-off place for the Big Santa Anita Canyon along which runs one of the Forest's most popular trails.

There is actually a paved road from Chantry Flats down into

the bottom of the Big Santa Anita, a road built to facilitate the construction of a large number of canyon erosion control dams. But the road is not used. Residents of the ninety-odd cabins in the canyon bottom must walk in. Users of organizational camps in the canyon walk in. Supplies—as large as refrigerators and as awkward as a bathtub—are hauled in by one of the few working pack strings in southern California and the only one in the San Gabriel Mountains.

This stable, of horses, mules and burros, operated by veteran mountain man Bill Adams, is located at Chantry Flats. In season the animals make as many as three daily trips down the hill into the canyon hauling food, fuel, luggage.

For the hiker here is the open door to all of the Angeles National Forest. Either a short hike or a long one is appropriate from this starting point. A fairly easy descent into the bottom of the Big Santa Anita brings into view the always-busy stream. Here is the junction with more precipitous Winter Creek, and further upstream, the Cascades.

From the Big Santa Anita it is possible to climb over Newcomb's Saddle into the West Fork of the San Gabriel River, and from there into the Charlton and Chilao country beyond. It is even possible from the Big Santa Anita trail to clamber up to Mt. Wilson. Several loop trips are possible. Before making long hikes on unfamiliar trails it is advisable to check with the ranger at the Chantry Flats Forest Service station. Actually this track is one of the best known in the Forest.

For those who enjoy less active sports there is room at Chantry Flats for walking, romping, picnicking, gazing down into the canyon depths or simply enjoying the sights and smells of the spiced chaparral forest. Small animals and mountain birds can be found in profusion. For all of its heavy day use, it is still a pleasant place.

From the world of the stone fist ax at the Southwest Museum, to the era of the Franciscan fathers at San Gabriel, down to the haunt of opossum and phoebe at the Audubon sanctuary and back to the palm-fringed lagoon at the Arboretum, this is a peaceful excursion into some of the best that the Southland has to offer.

These things command respectable audiences, and if you do not know them, you will find the meeting pleasant.

For some, sitting on a fallen log in the tangle of wild grape at the Audubon sanctuary watching the unplanned commerce of small birds offers a special reward.

As the gaps between houses grow smaller and open spaces become more precious, such rewards can only grow in value.

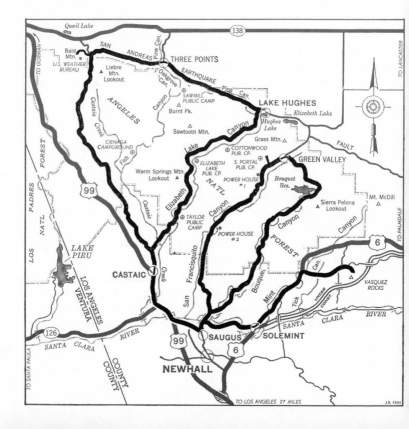

III THE CANYON COUNTRY NORTH OF NEWHALL

Fun to explore—best in the springtime
Length of exploration—allow several days for it all

THE SAN GABRIEL MOUNTAINS of Los Angeles County end in the sharp corner formed by the junction of the Ridge Route—U.S. Highway 99—and the San Andreas Fault line.

In this wedge of pleasant high country stands a handful of landmarks a mile high or thereabouts, with pine, spruce, live and black oak marching along the lofty runs of paved and unpaved roads.

Tucked into the canyons in this elbow of land is a quartet of byways that claim spectacular scenery, quiet charm, history and legends; it will take the average explorer more than one weekend to seek out all their hidden places. In the spring of the year, with a hint of timid green making its early show, with the black oaks beginning to put on leaf, it is an enchanting land of vernal freshness. It is unspoiled by heavy traffic, remote in some of its more pleasant aspects, and charming to almost everyone who calls.

Our byway starts at an improbable place: the highway-bypassed community of Castaic, an old ranch site that probably drew its place name from the Chumash Indians.

From Castaic the Elizabeth Lake Canyon road, now labeled Lake Hughes Road, runs toward the northeast. Not more than one mile out of Castaic a paved road, unmarked, bends off the highway to the left.

This is the Old Ridge Route, the almost-legendary, car-killing mountain nightmare of fifty years ago, which winds more than twenty-five miles before reaching State Highway 138 at the Quail

27

Lake fire station. Today it is all paved, seldom steep, almost never scary and, aside from other byway explorers, you'll have it entirely to yourself—except for one point where placid cattle graze across the right of way.

You will find many places where the narrow ribbon of concrete, laid down in 1914, still shows plainly; you'll find a few sections of the old 1914 wooden guard rail; but all the way stations like Tumble Inn and the National Forest Inn, Sandbergs and Old Reservoir Summit are gone.

From the ridge-running track you'll have a perfect view down into Violin Canyon to the west where the present Ridge Route sweeps along. Visible in many sections is the new super eight-laned freeway-like highway that will take the place of the two earlier Ridge Routes. You will also cross access roads to projects of the Feather River water project as you drive the Old Ridge Route.

The Old Ridge Route was built in 1914 and, including the awful run from Sandberg's to Grapevine, was: "forty-eight miles of narrow, tortuous mountain grades culminating in the hairpin turn of the infamous 'Deadman's Curve' in Grapevine Canyon."

The Grapevine section today is a model high-speed freeway. But the twenty-odd miles from Sandberg's to Castaic still sing the old song.

Even when the 1914 route across the end of the San Gabriels and into the Tehachapis was chewed out, engineers knew they could do better and were looking for another route.

It was slower cars and highway money that influenced the building of the 1914 ridge runner. Later the highway would be realigned, a dozen miles would be lopped off, it would be gradually widened to four and six lanes.

But that older highway was a winding nightmare. Along its 48.36 miles there were 39,441 degrees of curve, roughly 110

From Spunky Canyon Road the water level of Bouquet Canyon Reservoir looks very low

A glimpse of Antelope Valley from the Sawmill-Liebre dirt road dirt road which runs up above the Old Ridge Route

complete circles. Small wonder 1914-1929 drivers of the Ridge Route pulled off the road at the bottom of the grade and swore they'd never drive it again.

The new section of Ridge Route between Castaic and Gorman opened in 1933 and the snaking concrete ribbon became a ghost. The string of gas stations, resorts, tourist cabins disappeared, the "chain of bright lights that lit the Ridge Route from one end to the other" went out.

And still the changes continue in this canyon country. The new Ridge Route, a great brute of a highway, eight lanes wide, plus center strip and shoulders, will have a total width of 200 feet. It will just about split the avenue of real estate between the Old Ridge Route and the present highway. A highway built to take lots of punishment, with twelve-inch-thick reinforced concrete is what they plan. (The Old Ridge Route's narrow concrete ribbon was six inches thick and it still stands adjacent to more recent macadam that has weathered and worn into chuckholes and rubble.)

So this new mountain freeway will leave two Ridge Routes bypassed. The present highway will be given a chemical sealer coat and will be handed over to Los Angeles County for maintenance.

Up the Old Ridge, roughly twenty-five miles from Castaic, is a dirt side road leadng to the right, up Liebre Mountain. This is a narrow, switchbacked sometimes steep, sometimes rubbly, Forest Service truck trail. If you have mountain driving experience and are not dismayed by narrow mountain byways, take the side road. From the top of the 3.3-mile climb, at the Forest Service's West Liebre lookout, there is a magnificent view of about 270 degrees of canyon country to the south, west and north. To the east runs the long spine of mountain, the Sawmill-Liebre region, and from the lookout—which resembles an old windmill minus its vanes—a good mountain road runs east through chaparral, black oaks, scrub oaks, and pine to the Sawmill Campground spur, then, past the section of road that runs on to Lake Hughes, descends to the Pine Canyon Road just west of the Pine Canyon Ranger Station. Beyond Sawmill Campground bear to the left.

For those who are hesitant about tackling such a section of unpaved mountain road, the Old Ridge Route runs ahead from the Liebre Mountain turnoff, always an easy drive, past the site of Sandberg's resort, to the Quail Lake fire station and a four-way intersection.

The road to the west winds for a mile and a half up to the U.S. Weather Station atop Bald Mountain (visitors welcome). The road straight ahead leads to State Highway 138 and Gorman. We take the road to the east, the West Oakdale Canyon Road to Three Points, where junction is made with a lateral byway heading north again to Highway 138. From here we run on east, through buckeye country along Oakgrove Canyon on the Elizabeth Lake, Pine Canyon Road, past the point where our unpaved byway exploration came back to pavement, past the Pine Canyon Ranger Station, down to the pond of Hughes Lake and the community of Lake Hughes. Then the byway turns to the southwest along the second leg of our canyon-exploring trip, this time down Lake Elizabeth Canyon, or, as it is confusingly signed, the Lake Hughes Road.

According to interviews with some old-timers in the area, a wagon road of sorts existed in Elizabeth Lake Canyon as early as 1875. Other old-timers, however, argue that it wasn't until after the 1900's that a road worthy of mention ran up the canyon from Castaic to Lake Hughes. Certainly no mention was made of such a road in 1854 when Lt. Robert Stockton Williamson made his railroad survey.

It is twenty-one miles from Lake Hughes to Castaic along this canyon byway and the high point of its run is Cottonwood Forest Service Campground, about four miles south of Lake Hughes. This campground is one of the Angeles National Forest's newly reha-

*A spectacular view of Green Valley is enjoyed from
the top of Grass Mountain*

bilitated sites, with parking barrier to keep all cars out of camping and picnic areas, reducing the toll of human erosion.

Lying along the creek bottom, shaded by sycamores, willow and cottonwoods, with drinking water supplied by picturesque hand pumps, the campground is a pleasant and wait-a-while spot, heavily used by summer but beckoningly empty by winter and spring. It provides visitors with one of the Forest Service's new self-conducted nature trails where the hiker will be introduced to specific members of the chaparral family, native trees, geologic formations.

Elizabeth Lake Canyon Campground comes next on our southward meander down the pleasant canyon, roughly four miles distant, and beyond that the byway passes the Los Angeles County Department of Charities' Warm Springs Rehabilitation Camp where an unpaved side road runs west up Warm Springs Canyon into the Fish Canyon country and the recently burned-out Cienega Campground, once a great favorite with Scouters.

The Forest Service's Warm Springs lookout perches on a 4,020-foot peak high overhead.

On down the sinuous canyon we pass the Angeles National Forest's Elizabeth Lake Station, come to Taylor Campground, roughly seven miles from Castaic.

Some time around 1971 the Castaic Dam will be completed across the lower end of Elizabeth Lake Canyon. Part of the Feather River Project, the dam will hold back some 350,000 acre feet of water, ten times larger than the Bouquet Canyon reservoir, with canyon flooding reaching back over the Taylor Campground almost to the guard station.

A lake of nearly 2000 surface acres will then appear, requiring the rerouting and rebuilding of the Lake Hughes Road—which is the road down Elizabeth Lake Canyon—and either the rerouting or abandonment of the road up Castaic Canyon.

Back at Castaic we head south along U.S. Highway 99 to a junction with a road running east to Saugus. This we take, turn left at Saugus, continue on the short distance to Bouquet Junction, the place name marked on the store there. We leave what was once the beginning of the old Mint Canyon Road, and head north for about a mile and a half to a fork where San Francisquito Canyon Road bends to the west and Bouquet Canyon Road travels straight ahead. We take the westward-tending byway, into San Francisquito Canyon, past subdivision, school, scattered farms, back into the more primitive canyon country.

As you drive this peaceful, colorful canyon, slide back in time to March 12, 1928, over forty years ago.

Up ahead of you, spanning the canyon, is the two-year-old St. Francis Dam, part of the City of Los Angeles' water storage complex. The dam draws its name from the historic St. Francis Ranch which stood at the site. It is a big dam, 1,225 feet wide, 185 feet high. Behind it hangs between 36,000 and 38,000 acre feet of water from the Owens Valley.

Some of the canyon folks are worried about the dam. There has been talk of leaks in the dam face, hints that the concrete construction is faulty, rumors that the saturated footings of the dam are "mushy" with water.

It is after midnight, March 12, 1928.

There is a rumble, and then a roar, "like a truckload of pipe being driven past," and the two flanks of the dam crumble, a wall of water 185 feet high explodes down the canyon, wiping out before it the powerhouse, farmhouses, construction camps, Harry Carey's Indian Trading Post.

Ten miles below the ruptured dam, still in the quiet of darkness, the wall of water that hammers along is seventy-eight feet high.

Cars, houses, farms, farm animals, orchards are swept into rubble. The mounting loss of life, unknown in the night, will be shocking.

Four hundred homes in the sixteen-mile run of canyon from the dam to Piru are erased. "Not a standing timber is left," is the comment the following morning.

Three hundred homes are damaged at Santa Paula. Forty are wrecked at Fillmore. As the wall of water sweeps through Piru it is still forty feet high. It moves in the night all the way to the sea along the bed of the Santa Clara River, and on the edge of the ocean bridges are wrecked.

By 3:00 a.m. the horror is over. At the Southern California Edison camp at Piru a roll call accounts for only eighty out of 176 workmen.

In all, when the awful tally is made, upwards of 480 are dead or missing as a result of the disaster. Refugees are inoculated against typhoid. Thousands are recruited to clean up the wrecked homes, ruined orchards, dead animals.

Remember that night forty years ago as you drive up pleasant San Francisquito Canyon. You'll find a new Powerhouse No. 2 on the job now, and above it, at a narrows, a single knob of dun-colored masonry marks where that center section of the dam stood after the rupture. You might almost miss the landmark unless you look carefully. Off to the west side of the road it stands, in a spot now marked by many automobile tracks leading toward the stream and a brief row of trees.

The dam was never rebuilt. A short distance above the site stands a Los Angeles County detention camp where a crew of inmate workers is busy building a new road through upper San Francisquito Canyon. You'll drive on a small segment of this new, wider canyon road. Beyond, another section, not yet ready for paving, is being ripped from the west side of the canyon wall. This is a long-range highway program.

San Francisquito Canyon has known the march of wheels and hoofbeats for more than a hundred years. Lieutenant Williamson

At Vasquez Rocks, legend dictates, the infamous bandit Tiburcio Vasquez hid out after raiding in the Southland

Dun-colored rubble is all that is left of the St. Francis Dam

commented in 1854 that the San Francisquito Canyon Pass was then in common use. Other historians hint that a track stood here as far back as 1848, possibly even ten years earlier, catering to the comings and goings of gold seekers in this canyon country. Until the completion of the Old Ridge Route this was the way you crossed from Los Angeles to the San Joaquin Valley.

In the tree-shaded canyon bottom, you will come to a small settlement, a community gathered around impressive Powerhouse No. 1, a great collection of water-spun generators. The powerhouse is open to the public and should not be missed. It is an impressive sight, especially because of its remote canyon setting.

A short distance beyond Powerhouse No. 1 the paved road becomes unpaved, and it climbs stiffly up the west wall of San Francisquito Canyon. The road is narrow and winding, and you'll probably get few chances to look down into the great gorge at your side. Timid mountain drivers won't want to!

Then the road widens—though still unpaved—and levels. To the left a side road beckons, carrying a sign: South Portal Campground. Less than a mile off the main San Francisquito Canyon byway, South Portal Forest Service Campground is probably one of the most handsome in the area. Shaded extravagantly by giant live oaks, perched on ledges and flats above the small South Portal Canyon creek, the campground is delightful by spring, bursting with customers by summer.

A short distance beyond the campground notice the shell of a concrete building standing in a small open field. Just to its west (you can drive over almost to it) in the base of the canyon wall, is a big gated tunnel. This is a 1,300-foot access shaft back to the main tunnel that carries water from Fairmont Reservoir on the edge of the Antelope Valley down to Powerhouse No. 1.

There was a town of sorts here back in 1906, a town of 500 residents, workers on the great undermountain tube that ran from

Fairmont to San Francisquito Canyon. South Portal stood for about six years, and for those who wish to scramble around the now-chaparral-grown flats there are bits of broken crockery and other ghost town relics that mark a camp's passing.

Back on the main San Francisquito Canyon Road we enter pleasant, high, Green Valley—so called because of the many live oaks—with a permanent residency of about 420. The road forks, pavement resumes; straight ahead leads north to the Leona Valley Road, Elizabeth Lake, Munz Lake, Lake Hughes. To the right —the way we will go—the road winds through Green Valley, settled first around the 1890's and first called Dowd Canyon, toward the Bouquet Canyon Road.

On through Green Valley, we continue, past the fire-ravaged Spunky Canyon Forest Service Campground, and the road climbs, then descends a saddle just above Bouquet Reservoir, still another part of the Los Angeles City Department of Water and Power.

According to historical records Bouquet Canyon was known as El Potrero de Chico Lopez, and Deadman's Canyon, in the old days. Francisco Chari, a vaquero of Lopez's, had been a sailor before he settled in the canyon country. He constantly told his fellow vaqueros tales of "el buque," the ship he had sailed. Chari finally found himself being called "buque" and the canyon where he settled took the name from him. Subsequent careless cartographers and geographers corrupted the name from "buque" to bouquet.

Down Bouquet Canyon our byway leads us to The Falls, a cafe and store and a shady Forest Service campground. There is good rock-scrambling territory for youngsters, back to the steep, narrow spot in the canyon above the campground after which the site is named.

On down the canyon, past a series of shaded Forest Service campgrounds and cabins, the road continues in a most attractive deep canyon setting.

An unusual building commodity called Bouquet Canyon Stone comes from this area, and from nowhere else. Those desiring small quantities can apply at the district ranger station at Newhall for a permit (there is a small fee) and directions to a Forest quarry. There are also private quarries in the canyon where larger quantities are extracted and sold. Many of the cabins and summer homes are flanked, or otherwise decorated, with the multicolored flagstone.

Down, down, past a ranger station, past alder, sycamore, cottonwood and willow shading the stream, runs the Bouquet Canyon road. A strange ruddy outcropping of rocks known from the old days as The Pinnacles is passed, and shortly after that the canyon widens, past both abandoned and occupied farms back to Bouquet Junction.

East again we travel now, to Solemint Junction, then north along Mint Canyon, U.S. Highway 6, roughly six miles to Davenport Road.

Let us turn right along a fairly new road that has taken the place of that narrower, scarier road that was once the main access into the old Tick Canyon howlite collecting fields.

Tick Canyon crosses Davenport Road at the top of the grade. You'll recognize the place because of the large tailing pile of dark material along the road to the right, and to the left a narrow canyon opens. There is a short, dirt, dead-end road at this point that leads down to some crumbling concrete foundations, part of an old mill. This spot was, once upon a time, a great place for rockhounds to collect howlite: a grayish-white, easily workable gemstone that is usually made into such practical things as paperweights and bookends. Howlite is hard to find nowadays, but a scramble and search in the canyon is still fun. Other gemstones have been found in the area.

North is the intersection with the Agua Dulce Road, 3.3 miles from the Highway 6 turnoff.

A jog to the left, one to the right, then straight ahead for less than a quarter of a mile and we come to the entrance to Vasquez Rocks, southern California's most famous rock formation. The Vasquez Rocks area is now a county park, open only during daylight hours. At the rocks, where hundreds of motion pictures and TV films have been made, there are picnicking facilities. The old fort from the TV series "Bengal Lancers" still stands. Children will love climbing on the long slopes of rock, exploring the caves. The place name, of course, points to the legend that badman Tiburcio Vasquez used the site as a hideout.

Caretakers at the site, which was homesteaded by Henry Krieg, still find arrowheads and Indian grinding stones on the property.

It is a pleasant and historic site, fun for the whole family. At this point our byway exploration of the canyon country ends. Behind us, along Deadman's Canyon, past the ruins of the St. Francis Dam, up the twisted ribbon of the Old Ridge Route, out on Sawmill-Liebre and Grass Mountain's high places, there is scenery and history aplenty. That it is close at hand, a little more than an hour's drive from the main Los Angeles area, makes it that much more appealing. That it is still unspoiled gives the lie to the rumor that all of Los Angeles County is subdivided and settled.

There is still room to fire a sling shot in the Old Ridge Route country and not harm a thing. There is room to climb a rock and yell without being heard. Room to turn around, to stretch and breathe without being bumped into. Few excursions through Los Angeles County can boast more.

IV FROM PERRIS TO SAN JUAN CAPISTRANO

Fun to explore—some mountain areas closed in deep summer
Length of exploration—give it a full weekend

THERE IS SOME back country hidden in the purple green Elsinore Hills behind Murrieta that must look as pastoral California looked a hundred years ago. It is secreted from the average motorist only because it lies along an unpaved road.

This yesterday country, up behind the guardian ridge of the Elsinores, is mesa land, potrero country. Potrero is the Spanish word for "pasture ground." And this, largely, is what this liveoak-dotted flatland is devoted to: grazing land for cattle.

The road into the region is unpaved, but never difficult. And in the spring, granting the proper alchemy of rainfall and sunshine, the mesa land can be shindeep in green grass. Wildflowers may stand here: a whole spectrum of color ranging from the buttery yellow of California poppies to the sunset tones of Indian paintbrush.

A dip into this pleasant country is a bonus added to a byway adventure between the old Riverside County gold mining community of Perris, southwest across the Elsinore Mountains into San Juan Capistrano. There are other highlights for the explorer.

This byway trip starts at Perris, a town that came up in 1886. A settlement by the name of Pinacate stood two miles south before 1886, but the town moved north following a legal argument, and Fred T. Perris, a railroad engineer, gave his name to the new settlement.

It is fitting that the community had the railroad beginning. For

41

here today stands the Orange Empire Trolley Museum, an open air display of old streetcars and auxiliary electrics gathered from across half the world.

The Trolley Museum is located one mile south of Perris on A street. There are yellow Trolley Museum signs along the route through Perris to guide you to the site.

Here the visitor will find street cars—city cars, suburban cars and interurban cars—as well as maintenance vehicles: power car, crane car, shop switcher, flat cars, etc.—a locomotive, freight and observation cars. They have been gathered—bought and received as gifts—from such forgotten, little known, and no longer operating electric lines as the Bakersfield and Kern, the Fresno Traction, the San Diego Electric, the Visalia Electric, and the Pacific Electric Railway. All are in some process of restoration but many are in first-rate condition, looking almost as they did on their last days of operation.

The Orange Empire Trolley Museum was founded in 1956 by the Southern California Division of the Electrical Railroaders Association. The members' several pieces of rolling stock were assembled on the ten-acre plot purchased at Perris and the volunteer members went to work laying out track, installing overhead trolley wires, restoring the cars.

One car comes all the way from the Great Northern Railway in Eire; it was bought for $85, and cost $2,500 to have it shipped from Ireland. The oldest car on display was built in 1899, a former Los Angeles Pacific car that served as a trolley greaser in later years.

There is no admission charge to the Trolley Museum, which is open daily throughout the year. On Sunday afternoons lucky visitors are offered a short ride on one of the old trolley cars. At this time the excited members of the Museum fire up the local power plant, run a streetcar or the ponderous electric locomotive

*Visitors to the Orange Empire Trolley Museum at
Perris enjoy a ride on one of the old
electric trolley locomotives*

*Steep drop offs and overhanging rocks landmark
the road leading into DeLuz*

back and forth along a short length of track. This is heady wine for trolley buffs.

Groups wishing to make the Trolley Museum a site for more than casual study can arrange for a guide by writing in advance to the Orange Empire Trolley Museum, Perris, Calif. The Museum has had as many as 500 visitors in a day; some of the happiest of these have been retired trolley line employees from all over the country.

There is a small souvenir stand and office at the Museum where books and pamphlets on the subject can be purchased.

There is a dream, nourished by many Museum members, that someday track can be laid south from the Museum into the Railroad Canyon country, enough track to give visitors—and those eager members—a longer ride on the historic trolley cars.

Picturesque Railroad Canyon, reached via Newport Road off U.S. Highway 395, eight miles south of Perris, is the site of the old Railroad Canyon Reservoir once opened to the public but now a private recreation development.

On west of Railroad Canyon a freeway portion of State Highway 71 is crossed en route to Elsinore. Patience is a common commodity in Elsinore, for the lake, dry for so many years, finally was filled with purchased water, has in recent years enjoyed some of the joys of those earlier days when nature helped fill the big lake. There is camping, picnicking in the area. Elsinore has become noted in more recent years for a sky-diving center and a mecca for sailplaners.

On Palomar Street we head south out of Elsinore, continue on this byway that parallels State Highway 71, as its name changes from Palomar to Washington Avenue on the outksirts of Murrieta.

Here, on San Mateo Road, we turn right, toward the rim of mountains not far distant. Paved only for the first half mile after the turnoff, the San Mateo Road passes alfalfa fields, horse ranches, rural dwellings, and reaches the chaparraled Elsinore Mountains.

The climb up this edge of mountains is neither overly steep nor winding. The first summit is quickly gained and the attractive green bowl of mesa land opens to the west.

This is all cattle land, part of the Rancho California holding, a large development corporation which purchased the historic Vail Ranch here. While the byway is a county road, county maintained, the land to either side is private property and trespassing and hunting are prohibited.

Along this stretch the road runs level, climbs and dips only slightly on its run toward Tenaja. This is oak country and there are fourteen different varieties in the area. But the canyon live oak here assumes heroic size, casting a long shadow, shading the road, dotting the pale green meadowland with its deep olive-green bulk. Kingly sycamores also grow in this potrero region. Tar weed frequently puts on displays along the bottom land.

It is roughly twelve miles from Washington Avenue to Tenaja station. Our byway first gains a road junction with the right hand branch pointing to the Forest Service outpost. Then we enter the boundary of the Trabuco District of the Cleveland National Forest. A half mile from the road junction is the picturesquely fenced Tenaja Ranger Station and the Tenaja Forest Service Campground.

The campground, a favorite with Scouts and other outing groups, is situated among the boulders and oaks that flank beginning Tenaja Creek. Many of these large stones are marked with mortar holes, indicating that the Indians—they could have been either Juaneño or Luiseño—liked the acorns and water and probably the good hunting of the area. Arrowheads have been found nearby.

46

*The marshes around this pond—down Cottonwood Creek
from Tenaja—abound with croaking frogs*

On the opposite side of the ranger station are tie racks for horses, a facility of the Fallbrook Riding Club, which is also used by other equestrians.

The flatland driver will want to drive into Tenaja, picnic, maybe explore the great jumble of boulders along Tenaja Creek, and return the way he came, back over the handsome San Mateo Road.

Those with mountain driving ability who don't mind narrow, winding mountain roads, will want to drive on to De Luz via the attractive back country roads, a byway adventure of particular charm.

For this trip return to the road junction, a half mile from Tenaja, and turn right, to the west.

About a mile farther on, near the Johnson Ranch which sits off to the right, with some eucalyptus trees shading the old buildings, there is another junction.

Our byway takes a hard left here, along the road marked "Margarita Peak Lookout." A few yards down this road, at another fork, we turn left again, this time onto the De Luz Road. De Luz, by the sign, is seven miles away.

There is a brief stretch of potrero country here, some private ranches hidden behind coppices of oak and chaparral.

Then the road pinches in slightly, the turns are sharper, the grades are steeper. There is a spooky corner to duck around with a steep dropoff to the left, a great pale overhanging rock on the right.

Though it's downhill all the way to De Luz, it is a fairly gradual descent. There are some fine overlooks into the De Luz, Gavilan Mountain country to the southeast.

This is Cottonwood Creek we are bordering, and when the canyon bottom is reached the thickets of oak close in over the top of the road.

There is water, even a pond where frogs make a racket in their marshy hideouts. Pavement resumes and you pass a sign which informs you if you look back at it, that the way you have just come is not a through road.

Here is a junction, with a sign pointing east to Murrieta, twelve miles. Just beyond is a large two-story white house, and on its mailbox the sign "De Luz." That's all there is to the foothill community. Historian Erwin G. Gudde writes that the local tradition holds that an English settler named Luce built a large pen for his horses here and his Spanish neighbors called the site *Corral de Luz*. A post office was established in the 1880's but has not been active for many years.

At the Murrieta junction we turn eastward, pass the old De Luz school, leave the pavement, run through more of the attractive oak-covered stretches of road, climb and level, following De Luz Creek.

There are many pleasant vistas here: an abandoned farm with a patiently working windmill still standing sentry in a weed-grown field; a great windrow of white-barked eucalyptus; an old orange orchard; deep thickets of oak where the road ducks and hides.

Finally the byway climbs out of De Luz Creek, enters chaparral country, and in such a setting regains Murrieta.

North now we head, back up Washington Avenue-Palomar Street, to Elsinore and then west, on State Highway 74.

This byway sweeps south along the great wall of the Elsinore Mountains, as if reluctantly seeking an avenue up the great fault wall, then it turns sharply westward and begins to climb.

It is an easy ascent. Almost at the beginning of the climb the Cleveland National Forest is entered and signs along the route bear the names of the canyons: Slater Canyon, Guthrie Canyon, Edwards Canyon, Harlan Canyon, Brooks Canyon, etc., all

49

*Fine views of the Elsinore Valley are to be enjoyed
from the Ortega Highway*

named after Forest Service fire fighters who died in the terrible Decker Fire of 1959 in which six men were killed.

There are several view spots near the summit, Jameson Point and Ortega Terrace a pair of them. There is a snack bar and souvenir shop.

This stretch of State Highway 74 is called the Oretga Highway, built in 1929-1934, and named after José Francisco Ortega, a sergeant in the Portolá expedition into California in 1769.

The overlooks are breathtaking. On sparkling clear days it is possible to make out the individual features of the landmarks in the Elsinore Valley directly below. Beyond stretches the rumpled baize of hills that separates the Elsinore Valley from the Perris plain. Mt. San Jacinto is plainly visible.

Back from the sharp edge of the Elsinore Mountains, westward now, is the Forest Service's El Cariso Ranger Station and the El Cariso Campground.

The nearby highway summit—2,666 feet—explains why there are no conifers along this highest stretch of the Ortega Highway. But canyon live oaks are plentiful and they shade the modern campground. Before the Ortega Highway was built the area was used mostly for mining—the old Dominion Mine with many shafts and tunnels is nearby—and was reached by the old Perry Road which crawled up steeply from Elsinore.

The district ranger conducts the El Cariso Trek, a mile-long nature walk from the El Cariso ranger station, whenever enough interested visitors show up. He points out native plants and trees, mountain birds, the varied first prevention work being conducted by the Forest Service, examples of how man and nature can live together harmoniously. The trek takes about an hour, is an easy enough hike for all members of the family.

West down the Ortega Highway is the handsome Upper San Juan Campground. And here are the first scars of the 1958

Stewart Fire, a holocaust that took one life and burned 66,000 acres. The lower San Juan Campground is a smaller site.

The mountains are gentle here, soft, pastel and rolling, covered with the familiar aromatic chaparral. The San Juan summer home area is passed and the San Juan Guard Station at the old San Juan hot springs.

Then the byway rolls out of the Cleveland National Forest, follows still the opening canyon of San Juan Creek past sycamores, oak, willow and alder. There are tilled fields here, and cattle grazing. The buckwheat and sage draw bees and there are many apiaries.

Past the Mission Viejo Rancho the Ortega Highway ends at San Juan Capistrano, site of Mission San Juan Capistrano, founded in 1776.

Of all the twenty-one original Franciscan missions in California, this one, from the exterior, seems the most "touristy." It is the only one I can think of that has a souvenir shop directly across the street that sells "religious articles" and "sno cones."

Mission San Juan Capistrano is perhaps the most popular of all the missions and one of the reasons for this, of course, is the legend of the returning swallows—which depart from their mud-nests around the mission buildings on October 23 and return the following March 19. It is an incredible piece of folklore that ornithologists have long claimed is fiction. But swallows do seem to come and go on these dates in sufficient number to perpetuate the legend; a song has been written about them; ceramic swallow ashtrays are on sale at local souvenir shops; and determined ones can buy a music box that plays "When the Swallows Come Back to Capistrano."

An expert stonemason was hired to build a great domed church which was finished in 1806. In 1812 a stiff eathquake jarred the

52

mission community and destroyed the new church. The falling rubble killed forty Indians and the church was never rebuilt.

Services here are held in the smaller chapel, called Fr. Serra's little church.

The mission, completely walled and fenced, is entered through a gatehouse and souvenir shop, admission 50 cents, children under twelve free. Once inside there is a self-conducting tour (you are given a map and guide folder). The grounds are handsome, grown with vines, trees and shrubbery. There are pleasant fountains and, in addition to the swallows, there are dozens of white pigeons, here called doves, tame enough to eat grain from an outstretched hand.

The mission tour leads past the bell tower, the statue of Fr. Serra, the ruins of the old church, gardens, a more elaborate souvenir shop, a small museum, the chapel, the Indian cemetery, ruins of tallow vats, smelter, kitchen, workshops and a soldiers' barracks.

Let the byway adventure end here, inside the vined walls of San Juan Capistrano with the storied swallows making darting runs in the afternoon sky.

Behind you, up in the misty Santa Anas and Elsinores, up beyond the San Juan country, hide the old gold mines of the pioneers. Some say the mission fathers had a secret silver mine in the El Cariso region. Here is the haunt of coyote, fox, and rogue mountain lion; here deer know the secret trails to hidden springs.

This is a byway with the flavor of yesterday; at Perris's Trolley Museum, along De Luz's oak corridors; in the cool archways at San Juan Capistrano. And this is the charm of the country.

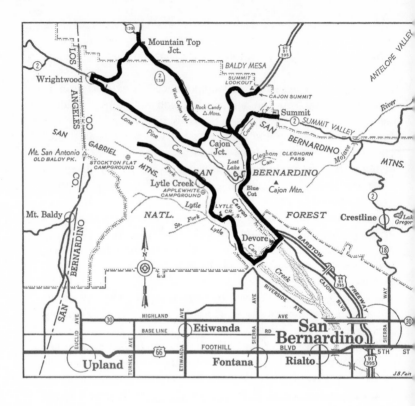

V THROUGH HISTORIC CAJON PASS

Fun to explore—any time of the year
Length of exploration—can be driven in a day

FROM THE TOWER atop bald Cajon Mountain the Forest Service lookout can see all the secrets of San Bernardino County's broken Cajon country. It spreads out a half mile below in a rumpled gray and purple and brown tapestry: Lytle Creek, Devore, Lone Pine Canyon, the Rock Candy Mountains, West Cajon Valley, Baldy Mesa, Summit Valley, back into the Cleghorn region. Below are the varnished worms that travel the silvery rails, and the ants that work the freeway—trains and automobiles are no larger from the lookout's perch at 5,340 feet. By afternoon smog may elbow into the Cajon from the south, muting the colors, making it difficult to spot small smokes, paring down visibility. By night, with the freeway procession transformed into a ribbon of undulating lights, the view from the lookout is exhilarating.

This is the lookout's personal world, real yet remote. With his spotting scope he can see the features of individuals stopped along the freeway. But he is more at home with the deer that browse on Cajon Mountain's bare top by sunset and the hawk, moving in great swinging arcs out in the warm and buoyant uplifts from Cajon's slopes.

Cajon is the Spanish word for box. Box canyon, then, is the meaning of this place name, this valley that separates the San Bernardino Mountains on the east from the San Gabriel Mountains on the west. It was Padre Joaquin Pascual Nuez in 1819 who officially named the place. In his diaries it was called *ex-Caxon de San Gabriel de Amuscopiabit*. Amuscopiabit, or Muscupiavit, is the name of the old Indian rancheria here.

If Padro Fages used the Cajon for his crossing here in 1772 instead of the old Mojave Trail which climbed the mountains to the east, then he was the first white man to traverse the canyon. It was known that Father José María Zalvidea crossed this way during an expedition into the Mojave region in 1804. And the first American would have been the colorful mountain man Jedediah Strong Smith who came west from Salt Lake City in 1826-27, crossed the desert from the Colorado River at the Needles and entered the San Bernardino Valley via the Cajon.

After that came the probable crossing by the Antonio Armijo party, trappers Ewing Young and William Wolfskill. Still the first wheel had yet to roll across the Cajon's rocky terrain.

That came in 1848, when a group of soldiers from the Mormon Battalion made the crossing. Jefferson Hunt brought a caravan of wagons into the San Bernardino Valley in 1849.

Traffic began to increase then. Freighting developed through the Cajon. Lt. Edward Beale came through the Cajon with his incredible caravan of camels in 1857, and later that year the railroad survey through the canyon was made by Lt. R. S. Williamson. Williamson's survey steered the course of the railroad out into West Cajon Valley, extricated it from the head of the box canyon via a 3.4-mile tunnel.

By now the trickle of traffic through Cajon Pass had grown to a small flood. In the great migration of 1851 more than one way to enter the canyon from the north was used: even today historians do not agree on which was the favorite route. It was the 1875 boom at Panamint City in the Panamint Mountains to the north that spurred work on Lt. Williamson's idea of a railroad tunnel in the West Cajon Valley. A mile or so of roadbed was graded, the

Some of the best country in the San Bernardinos is up on Sugar Pine Mountain—just east of Cajon Pass

drilling of the tunnel was started. Then the boom at Panamint City turned to bust, work on the project stopped, the site was abandoned.

The Cajon railroad idea was quiet until 1879 when engineers became convinced that a route could be found that would avoid the costly tunnel. The work started and by 1885 Santa Fe trains were rolling through the Cajon. The era of wagon freighting was over. The county took over the toll road, made the route into a free road, and in time made it a state highway.

Exploring the Cajon country is a sentimental journey in a way, for in the crossing as much history as geography is traced.

A freeway reaches up into the Cajon now from the south, the arm of an arterial that stretches uninterrupted all the way into Los Angeles. Drive north out of San Bernardino on that freeway, but turn off to the left at Devore—into gold country.

Camped in the mouth of this tributary canyon in 1851 was Andrew Lytle, captain of one of three Mormon companies that made the crossing from Salt Lake City that year. In 1857, settlers in the canyon—which took Lytle's name—were the Wixom brothers, Dave H. and Willard Silas Glenn and his family made a home in Lytle Creek in 1867. In the 1860's gold was discovered. Miners made as much as $40 a day from placering along the Lytle Creek sandbars. Even as late as 1890 there were 100 miners in the area, making only $4.00 a day, but even that was wages.

James S. Banks founded the famed Hocumac Mine at the head of Lytle Creek. A flood in 1891 ended most mining in Lytle Creek—the activity moved over the Baldy Notch into San Antonio Canyon. But weekend prospectors still try their luck at panning the flour gold from the streams coming down the South and Middle Forks of Lytle Creek.

As you near the Lytle Creek narrows there is a great scar on

58

the west where limited hydraulicking was done in the early days. Beyond the narrows—note the old prospect holes right along the road—the canyon opens, the new Lytle Creek Ranger Station, headquarters of the San Bernardino National Forest's Cajon District, is passed. The road reaches back to summer home tracts—many of these are permanent, year-round dwellings—resorts and the sprawling Applewhite Forest Service campground. Water runs in the stream here, even in a dry autumn. Beyond the camping and picnic areas the pavement ends, but an interesting, if chuckholed once-paved road reaches up Lytle Creek into the Stockton Flats country to a small campground which will be enlarged in the future.

The Cajon freeway, north from Devore, closely parallels the railroad. To the west was the vanished railroad station of Keenbrook. From a turnout here it is possible to look west across the streambed and see the crumbling masonry of an old kiln or smelter against the hill. This smelter, some residents claim, was once used in the processing of gold ore. There are stories of gold mines in nearby canyons. Others say that the kiln burned limestone quarried in the area.

Past Keenbrook the highway enters the narrow gorge of Blue Cut, flanks Lone Pine Canyon reaching off toward the northwest. Just up Lone Pine Canyon from the Cajon is tiny Lost Lake, an oddity in this arid country.

In the stream bottom here up from the old campground, the patient naturalist can find a series of beaver dams: a strange locale for the shy beaver, between the streamliners' rails and the modern freeway.

The historic old railroad station of Cajon is gone now, torn down and hauled away. There is a tall water tank at Keenbrook; even the water tank has been removed at Cajon.

Beyond, on the east side of the freeway, a side road leads up

59

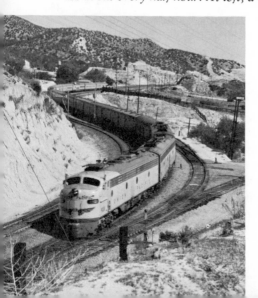

Forest Service lookout watches for fire from atop Cajon Mt.

Both freight and passenger trains rumble through Cajon Pass about every half hour. At left, a UP streamliner

into Crowder Canyon, Summit Valley and on east. Here is the actual Cajon Pass, but those who never leave the freeway miss the geographical landmark. The summit here is the high point of the Santa Fe and Union Pacific crossings of the Cajon. There are several vantage points from which it is possible to photograph the slow-moving freight and passenger trains that rumble past about every twenty or thirty minutes.

From Summit this side road runs east of Cedar Springs, where, when the Feather River project is developed, a great reservoir and dam will be constructed and developed for recreational use.

Returning to the Cajon freeway—U.S. Highways 66 and 395, plus Interstate 15—we pass a Forest Service fire suppression station and come to the junction of State Highway 138 from the west. We take this side road, cross two bights of track, and enter the Rock Candy Mountains.

Sandstone, but still spongy-looking, the Rock Candy Mountains beg to be explored. Pocked by wind and weather, the outcropping lies on either side of Highway 138. A couple of jeep tracks lead off toward the major pile of sandstone hills to the north and cross the streambed of West Cajon Canyon wash. Don't trust your passenger car in this sandy, gravelly area. Better park and walk the short distance out to the rocks to explore those caves. All manner of small animals and bird life is here, and by season even a shy tarantula can be found—furry, timid and harmless. In recent years the Rock Candy Mountains have been called by an older name, the Mormon Camp Rocks. The new Forest Service Ranger Station—the old Cajon Station—is located on the south side of the road here and is called the Mormon Rocks Station.

Beyond the Rock Candy Mountains, and past the side road into Lone Pine Canyon, the highway continues up West Cajon Valley toward Mountain Top Junction. To the north, against the south face of Baldy Mesa, may be seen the rough outlines of the roadbed of the 1875 railroad and tunnel access built when Panamint City was booming. It is possible to walk along the mile or so of the route of what might have been a railroad from Los Angeles into the Panamint Valley. The mouth of the partly dug tunnel is choked with fallen rock and impossible to distinguish now.

Highway 138 brings you to Mountain Top Junction where a turn to the left leads back a short distance to Wrightwood. From Wrightwood, in Swarthout Valley, you can drive on to the Holiday Hill ski area, the Big Pines region, and the winter sports areas at Table Mountain and Blue Ridge.

It is possible to make a loop drive from Cajon Junction to Wrightwood and return using the less traveled but paved route of Lone Pine Canyon as one side of the circle.

Back at Cajon Junction we head on north, climbing now, past a brush conversion project of the San Bernardino National Forest, to Summit lookout. Operated by the State Division of Forestry, this vantage point offers views of the Baldy Mesa country and the route of the Santa Fe and Union Pacific as they climb into Summit and Summit Valley to the southeast. Fires have been frequent along the railroad right of way, but strong agency cooperation has reduced many of the natural hazards.

The Summit lookout is open to the public and the veteran smoke spotter there will be happy to explain the names of the geographic features of the area. To the east are the Pinnacles and Pilot Rock—the latter served as a landmark for the early travelers who used the old Mojave Trail. Out this way, blending and blurring with the hazy San Bernardinos, are the Ord Mountains.

At Summit lookout gusty winter winds—the Santa Ana—can whip up velocities as high as 83 miles per hour. The elevation of 4,400 feet is frosty by deep winter.

From this point the freeway runs northeast toward its rendezvous with Victorville and Barstow out in the Mojave Desert. Side roads lead to Hesperia, Apple Valley, Lucerne Valley along this route.

Closed to the public yet worthy of mention, is the mountain region up from Cajon Pass to the east, the country under the scope of Forest Service lookout in his Cajon Mountain eyrie. A net of dirt roads, Forest Service truck trails, cross and recross private land in such a bewildering fashion that the Forest Service cannot at this time offer unlimited access to the public. In time, according to hopeful Forest Service plans, some of these problems may be worked out. Then, perhaps, it will be possible to visit the deep woods country high on the side of Sugarpine Mountain, where there are lonely avenues of ponderosa pine and incense cedar, baked by summer suns and stirred by winter winds until the whole mountainside is deep in pine duff and rich with aromatic, resinous smells. Here are the tracks of bear and bobcat, coyote and mountain lion. Closed on one side much of the year because of fire hazard, sealed off on the other because of difficult access, the deep mountain country offers half a dozen sites that would be idyllic campgrounds or picnic areas. The brake fern grows man high and rattlesnakes sun themselves unafraid by lonely springs. Across this region passed the old Mojave Trail, the route from the Mojave River over the ridges and down into the San Bernardino Valley. On a hogback, flanked by Cable Canyon on the west and Devil's Canyon on the east, there is a monument to the old Mojave Trail.

This, then, is the Cajon country. It has known the hoof of the pack animal, the steps of the trapper and Franciscan explorer; it has known the spirit level of the railroad surveyor and the pick of the prospector. Today, riven by steel rails and concrete freeway, it still presents a yesterday air with its beaver dams, its forgotten rock kilns, its moody Rock Candy Mountains. The San Andreas

Fault lies here, and because of its awesome presence, perhaps it is well that no railroad tunnel ever pierced Baldy Mesa.

You can drive the San Bernardino Freeway from the south end of the Cajon to Summit Lookout in a few minutes. But to see the Cajon country—Lytle Creek, Lone Pine Canyon, the Rock Candy Mountains, Summit Valley, West Cajon Valley, the haunt of streamliner and skier, will take a full, rich day.

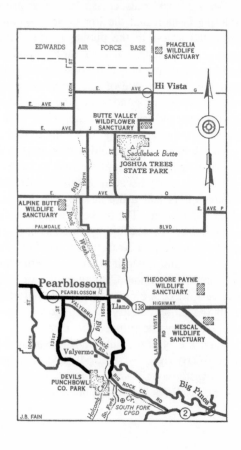

VI INTO THE DEVIL'S PUNCHBOWL COUNTRY

Fun to explore—any time of the year
Length of exploration—can be driven in a day

IF YOU COULD call any spot in the mountains of southern California a *tanglewood,* this would surely be the place.

Full of wait-a-while brambles, dead-end canyons, shadowed waterfalls, rock chutes, sand and thickets of clutching dead branches, the bottom of the Devil's Punchbowl is a classic tanglewood.

And this, of course, is the charm of the place.

It used to be a two-mile hike from the South Fork Campground on Big Rock Creek to get to the mile-high Devil's Punchbowl country. Still, many made the climb.

Will Thrall, pioneer mountain man who explored on foot all there was of the San Gabriel Mountains, rejoiced when the Forest Service hacked out the new trail from the South Fork (then Holcomb) Campground in 1935. Before that it had been pretty much a cross-country scramble.

"Stay two days," he urged hikers. "You can't see it any faster than that," Thrall, like other early arrivers, brought home fist-sized rocks filled with fossils, marine fossils reaching back into a time when the Punchbowl conglomerate was the ooze on the bottom of some prehistoric sea.

The 1935 trail was the route into the Punchbowl for almost thirty years. In 1963 the Los Angeles County Department of Parks and Recreation dedicated the Devil's Punchbowl County Park, opened a brand new 2.5-mile access road across the high desert-foothill country almost to the edge of the strange depression, and invited the public to come and look.

The Devil's Punchbowl is described technically as a "structural depression lying between the San Andreas Fault on the north and the Punchbowl and San Jacinto Faults on the south." The activity along these faults is responsible for the unusual geological formations.

In Tertiary times marine, and later continental sediments, were deposited in this depression. The layers were thick—up to 10,000 feet. By faulting action these sediments were compressed and folded, broken and lifted, separated and shifted until now the great bowl is filled with sheaves of layered rock, like playing cards standing on edge, tilted, weathered, broken, crumbling, forming parallel canyons and watercourses; some stone planes are lifted above the horizon and slanted, others are still hidden below the lip of the bowl.

There are perhaps three lateral miles of Punchbowl formation here along the San Andreas. Some geologists feel that the Rock Candy Mountains formation, near Cajon Junction, are part of the same formation. These rocks lie on the opposite side of the earthquake fault. North-south slippage has resulted in the two outcroppings being some twenty air lines apart. An air view of the area clearly shows the fault line.

Because of their age, the Punchbowl rocks are strange. In some places the sedimentary rocks look like great slices of a fancy pudding. Small varicolored rocks are imbedded in the pink sandstone, and these have been eroded, weathered and polished until it looks like the pudding was sliced with a sharp knife.

Remains of ancient animals which lived here about thirteen million years ago have been found in the pink sediments of the Punchbowl formations of Miocene age. These include two species of the

The geological formations of the Punchbowl are only part of the area's attraction . . . wildlife is abundant here too

three-toed horse, an ancient skunk-like animal, a primitive camel, and a small antelope.

There have been reports of prehistoric animal footprints in the rocks of the Punchbowl, but these accounts have largely been discounted. It is easy to "see" such prints in the worn sandstone. For years such footprints were known to exist in the Anza-Borrego area but these were finally proven to be weatherings in the soft rock of the Split Mountain region.

Beds of coal and algal limestone also occur in portions of the Punchbowl. And overlaying much of the Punchbowl formation are poorly sorted, unconsolidated gravels and silt.

The Los Angeles County Park and Recreation Department's interest in the Devil's Punchbowl dates back to 1949. It was not until a field trip into the region in August of 1957 that enough interest was aroused to secure official aproval of the site and the county was advised to investigate the feasibility of building a public road into it.

The Forest Service agreed to a special use permit involving 1,270 acres of Punchbowl land; orders went out to purchase forty acres of private land in the area, the access road was given a high priority; and the Regional Planning Commission smiled on the project.

Then, on June 11, 1958, the whole project stalled. The county Board of Supervisors wanted assurances from federal and state agencies that they weren't interested in developing the Punchbowl as a recreation area. DeWitt Nelson, director of the state's Department of Natural Resources, assured the county that the state had no designs on the Punchbowl, but thought "in the judgement of our investigators the suitability for public recreation on a county or regional basis is unquestioned."

So the county started up the machinery of development again. On December 4, 1963, the park was opened and dedicated.

The dedication ceremonies were followed by a steak barbecue. A descriptive plaque was placed here by the Automobile Club of Southern California.

There is a 50-car parking lot at the end of the access road. The last section of the road is gravelled, not paved, with an eye to keeping the spot a little more rustic than a city park.

The cement block residence perched on the edge of the bowl, formerly owned and occupied by the Charles Guys of Northridge, is now the headquarters for the park director. An attractive low rail fence guards the steeper approaches to the bowl.

Not a part of the park at all, and prohibited to visitors, is a forty-acre section to the north of the county preserve. This is the Blanche Folkes Hamilton Wildlife Sanctuary, a gift to the Nature Conservancy, a national conservation organization, by Southlander J. F. Hamilton.

With the permission of the Forest Service and water authorities, Hamilton has constructed a dam across Sandrock Creek to provide water for the abundant wildlife here throughout the year.

Here conservationist Hamilton has seen deer, coyote, fox, bobcat, rabbit, squirrel, many kinds of bird life including small owls that use the crannies of the Punchbowl's weathered rocks for nesting places. Mountain lion tracks have been seen in the bowl area.

The Blanche Folkes Hamilton Wildlife Sanctuary will thus become a kind of living museum. There are no structures, no permanent roads on the property. It will be kept in as wild a state as possible. As much as the county wants visitors to use their portion of the Devil's Punchbowl, Hamilton and the Nature Conservancy wants only undisturbed birds and animals in their part of the region. If the two ideas prove to be compatible—and both sides hope for this—it will be an outstanding example of how recreation and conservation can go hand in hand in a relatively small area.

To get to the Devil's Punchbowl from the Southland, drive north

*Tilted, broken and shifted; slanted, folded and lifted—this
is the Punchbowl*

toward the Antelope Valley arm of the Mojave Desert either over U.S. Highway 6 and the Antelope Valley Freeway, or over the Angeles Forest Highway, to the Littlerock turnoff just north of Vincent. The turnoff is signed.

Follow this road east, which becomes State Highway 138 at Littlerock, to the community of Pearblossom. Turn south here at 131st Street and go to 4.5 miles to a road leading east called Tumbleweed Road. This is the new county road. From this point in the Juniper Hill country you can look east and see the blades of rock of the Punchbowl formation standing above the horizon. To your south is Pleasant View Ridge, and behind it, the bulk of Mt. Baden-Powell, Mt. Lewis and Mt. Williamson.

Drive east on Tumbleweed Road to the Punchbowl park area.

If you wish to follow the old 1935 trail into the Punchbowl, drive on east past Pearblossom on State Highway 138 to 165th Street, turn south through Valyermo and pick up the Big Rock Creek road just beyond the ranger station. Follow the paved Big Rock Creek road 2.5 miles to the turnoff into the South Fork Forest Service Campground. There is a mile of good dirt road leading into the camping area. Park here and take the signed trail up over the ridge and down into Holcomb Canyon and thence into the Punchbowl. You'll see a side trail pointing off to the west to the Devil's Chair. If you are a sturdier hiker, add this strange rock formation to your collection of sights gathered.

No trip to the Devil's Punchbowl should be made without a glimpse of the fascinating Antelope Valley area immediately to the north. Hard by the Punchbowl region is the vanished utopian colony of Llano, or, as it was originally known, Llano del Rio.

It was in 1914 that Job Harriman formed the colony here, bought stock from the almost-defunct Mescal Water and Land Co., and started the faithful moving onto the plot. The members of the Llano plan were largely socialists or labor union members.

71

The rapidly vanishing Joshua tree is being protected at 2,721-acre Joshua Tree State Park

Tent and adobe structures went up. A few cobblestone buildings were erected. It cost $500 to join the colony and many did.

The colony had secured water rights to Big Rock Creek. With water crops grew. Hand labor—hard hand labor—tore away Joshua trees and mesquite and creosote bush. Alfalfa flourished. Corn was raised. Pear orchards were less successful. There were 2,000 acres under cultivation in 1917. The colony produced as much as 90 percent of the food it required. Women of the colony made handicraft items such as rag rugs and, in spite of terrible transportation problems, these were exported.

Internal problems began to gnaw at the utopian colony's structure. Members argued with Harriman and withdrew. The water supply for Big Rock Creek was disappointing. Plans developed to move the colony to west-central Louisiana where it would be called Newllano. Through mismanagement the Antelope Valley colony was forced to declare bankruptcy and it was ordered closed by the courts in 1918.

There is little to see of old Llano del Rio today. Only old-timers know the empty fields where cobblestone ruins doze. Still it is a fascinating page of California's history, one that should not be forgotten.

North of the Pearblossom-Llano area 165th Street runs north, jogs to the right at Palmdale Boulevard, continues north on 180th Street, jogs west briefly at Avenue O and continues north again on 170th Street to Joshua Trees State Park, a 2,721-acre preserve set aside by the state to protect the vanishing Joshua tree.

Once the Joshua trees crowded in close to both Palmdale and Lancaster, thick forests of the trees stood here but the bulldozer and the subdivider have cleared the land of these. The state park under the shadow of lonely Saddleback Butte is a Joshua tree sanctuary. Here the giant supplicating trees will be undisturbed, and generations of Californians after us will be able to see how these strange desert plants grew in the wild state.

This corner of the Antelope Valley is a region of many moods. On a chill winter day, late in the afternoon when clouds gather together, there is a spell on the land.

Colors then run mostly to purples and velvety rose. The San Gabriel Mountains to the south are a silhouette of blue-black. The parade of buttes across the floor of the Antelope Valley here— Alpine Butte, Lovejoy Butte, Rocky Butte, Black Butte, Saddleback—have a long-shadowed lunar aspect. Some of the meaner homes along here have a melancholy cast about them. An abandoned gasoline stations seems more a sad, neglected movie set than a former habitation.

Yet in the early morning brilliance the many subtle colors of the land become alive: Buffs and duns and pastels beyond counting. Old landmarks seem new; distances seem exciting and inviting. This kind of contrast is the charm of the desert—always changing, always different, always powerful enough to affect more than the most obvious senses.

In the area between the Punchbowl and Joshua Trees State Park are five county wildflower sanctuaries where, almost throughout the year, some kind of bright blossom—perhaps only tiny ones— can be found. In the warm flood of first spring the fields here are brilliant with poppy and paintbrush. Nearby Hi Vista has an annual wildflower celebration.

The blossom preserves are: Butte Valley Wildflower Sanctuary, 320 acres; Alpine Butte Wildflower Sanctuary, 320 acres; Theodore Payne Wildflower Sanctuary, 320 acres; Mescal Wildflower Sanctuary, 100 acres; and Phacelia Wildflower Sanctuary, 100 acres. All contain Joshua trees; in the Alpine Butte site experts have found a fifty-five-foot giant.

For all its rural charm, this section of Los Angeles County is not well known. Antelope Valley folks are casual confidants with the secrets of the land, but this back side of the San Gabriel Mountains is little explored by basin dwellers.

Because of the Punchbowl, I predict that this country will see many new visitors. They will come because of the Devil's Punchbowl, because it is a wildland, mysterious in the play of sun and shadow in the great depression; they will be held by the call of bird, the flash of squirrel and rabbit; the shadow of fox and coyote. They will come because of the noisy little stream that works here and they will come back because of its secret meanderings. They will come to ponder the slanting tables of rough stone, immense and unreadable.

Mostly they will come because here is unconventional scenery—unspoiled, untracked, unlimited—where they can invest a day of looking and hiking and savoring the uncommon geography: Punchbowl, Joshua trees, buttes.

And they will envy Will Thrall who came and stayed as long as he wanted in the hospitable country.

Small rills and waterfalls, such as the one at right, can be discovered here and there throughout the Park

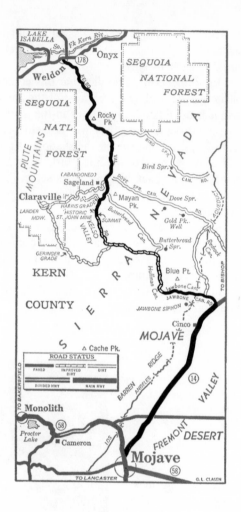

VII THROUGH THE KELSO VALLEY

Fun to explore—all but the high mountain portion
can be driven any time of the year. Warm by summer
Length of exploration—can be driven in a day

A FISHNET OF ROADS, paved and unpaved, fans out from the mouth of Jawbone Canyon in eastern Kern County and ensnares some of the most pleasant and peaceful foothill and mountain country in the lower Sierra Nevada.

The main course through this tangle is the Jawbone Canyon Road, for as long as it maintains that identity, and after that it's the Kelso Valley Road. From the beginning at State Highway 14, twenty-odd miles north of Mojave, the Jawbone Canyon Road-Kelso Valley Road takes the byway explorer northwest to Weldon on State Highway 178 east of Lake Isabella.

There are a score or more places where you can turn off this main avenue through the rabbit brush, sage and Joshua trees. By summer and winter you'll find these little side canyons and spur roads dotted with campers, trailers and tents of those Southlanders who would get away from the press of city life for even a weekend. This is good getting-away-from-it-all country. The air here, from 2000 feet up to 5000 feet elevation, has an herb-scented bite to it. The rabbit brush and the sage add spice to the wind, and the scrub pines that stand along the eastern face of the Piute Mountains add a medicinal flavor.

There is a summit here, just under a mile high, from which you can see for miles out to the east. The Rand Mountains march along the far edge of the horizon and north of them the black-topped

—Department of Water & Power

*An early photograph of Jawbone Siphon (taken between 1908
and 1913 when this marvel of engineering was being built)
shows the old construction camp on the valley floor*

El Pasos shoulder the sky. In the country nearer at hand, Koehn Dry Lake and Saltdale make a showing on the plain. The green patches are alfalfa growing out across Fremont Valley. The sprawl of the Mojave Desert reaches away to the south.

The logical place to start this adventure is at State Highway 14 north of Mojave. The Jawbone Canyon—Kelso Valley turnoff is plainly marked.

Historian Richard C. Bailey, of the Kern County Historical Society, says the name "Jawbone Canyon" comes from the discovery by early prospectors of a fossil jawbone. Erwin G. Gudde, place name expert, says that Jawbone Canyon is so named because it is shaped like a jawbone. Either way, it is a colorful title for an attractive desert canyon.

Two miles west of Highway 14 is an intersection with a good paved road reaching to the north. If you have a high-clearance passenger car or a pickup or jeep, you might wish to pursue this side road back up to a point behind Redrock Canyon.

Three miles inland is the crossing of the Jawbone Siphon of the giant Los Angeles Aqueduct. The Jawbone Siphon was one of the engineering marvels of the aqueduct project, built between 1908 and 1913. In the final report of the project it is written that the Jawbone project employed a build-up pipe 36 feet 10 inches long, weighing 52,000 pounds—26 tons. From the railroad junction at Cinco the great segment of pipe was hauled to the canyon site by means of a fifty-two-mule team.

Today the giant pipe—seven and a half feet in diameter—is just as impressive as it was fifty-five years ago. That it has weathered the extremes in winter and summer temperature here on the edge of the Mojave Desert is a testimony to the quality of the early-day engineering.

Just west of the siphon crossing is the residence of the local aqueduct tender.

79

*Some thoughtless plinkers have made a mess of the road
signs in the Kelso Valley area*

The good paved road continues west and the canyon opens slightly. Freighting wagons once traveled this way enroute to mines in the Piutes but there is no trace of them today.

An outcropping of greenish stone off to the north has earned the name of Blue Point. From it a large quantity of roofing stone is quarried.

Numerous side canyons are passed where campers and trailers seek foothill solitude. Harmless snakes live here, lizards, rabbits, ground squirrels and colorful roadrunners.

The road forks and we tend toward the right. Pavement ends but the dirt road is well-bladed and smooth as it starts to climb to the north parallel to Hoffman Canyon.

In a few minutes we reach some of the spectacular vistas to the east. The road stretches ahead like a broad dun ribbon. Dwarf Joshua trees have put in an appearance.

At last the summit is gained and Kelso Valley, eight miles long and three miles wide, opens suddenly. Part of the roadside graze is fenced by cattle raisers. The Piute Mountains lift directly to the west, darkened with stands of pine and oak. Some junipers in the Valley are mixed with the forest of Joshua trees.

The Jawbone Canyon road, from the junction with the Kelso Valley route, continues west up the infamous Geringer Grade into the Piutes. A short spur road runs south to some old mining properties.

We take the Kelso Valley Road north, through Joshua trees and grazing cattle toward a low summit.

Here, according to Bailey, is the site of the historic old St. John Mine, an operation that dates back to 1867. The tailings from the eight claims of the gold producer lie on either side of the highway.

Bailey recounts a report in the old *Havilah Courier* on March 21, 1868, stating "the St. John Mine, at a clean-up some weeks since, obtained $7,500 after a week's run. The company obtained

81

*The deserted old tungsten mill on the outskirts of Weldon
was once a busy producer*

*Plows have left brown furrows on the land that will be
green with grains and grasses by spring*

$9,000 at the clean-up, after a fortnight's run." The mine was active until the 1940s, was finally abandoned when water seeped into the diggings. Numerous collapsed shafts require caution by explorers on foot.

The dirt road becomes paved again as it winds and twists toward Mayan Peak. To the east is the Butterbread Canyon road back toward Butterbread Spring and Jawbone Canyon.

Then at a main junction is the site of abandoned Sageland. West from this outpost, once called the "trading center for the New Eldorado mining district," runs the Harris Spring Grade road up into the Piute Mountains. This is a dirt road and steep at times, but in fair weather, and when there is no snow on the ground, it can be driven by passenger cars. The last time we traveled it a great army of motorcycle riders were challenging the Harris Springs Grade giving additional spice to the ascent of the narrow mountain road. Up the grade nine and a half miles, just beyond Lander Meadow, is old Claraville.

Unhappily, not a single building is left to mark this once booming mountain town. Until recent years there remained an old wooden building, built with pegs and square nails. It is said that it was the old justice courthouse, built in the 1860s. It has been dismantled, hauled to Bakersfield's fine Pioneer Village and put together again. At least it is saved from the vandals, but a ghost town without a single building to be haunted is a sad thing.

Prospectors still poke around in the gravels nearby. Bottle hunters armed with metal locators have dug here. The grazing cattle are the most peaceful of the visitors. Historian Bailey recounts that Claraville was named for Clara Munckton, the first white girl in camp. As early as 1869 the boom camp had faded. In the June 22 *Havilah Courier* of that year a visit to the site is described: ". . . we passed the site of Claraville, once a beautiful village, but now totally deserted—over a dozen houses, neat and comfortable in their appearance without a solitary tenant."

A walk north from the road, over the site of Claraville to the low ridge of hills, is rewarding. Several spots where Indian mortar holes can be found in the rocks indicate that the aboriginal people liked the summertime site of Claraville every bit as much as the miners who came later.

But, remember, this climb up the Harris Spring Grade is not recommended in bad weather or even just after bad weather. If the sun is smiling and if it has been that way for some days, take the chance. But you'll find few turnouts—places to change your mind—on that nine-and-a-half-mile climb.

There was once a store and gasoline station at Sageland. It was called Shorty's Place and you can still make out the sign on the old building that is left. But is just a shell now. Sageland is gone and you'd need an expert to help you find the old cemetery hidden away in the brush.

Less than a mile beyond Sageland branches the Dove Springs Canyon road which runs down to Highway 14 via Dove Springs and Gold Peak Well.

A flinty outcropping known as Rocky Point is passed. There are fewer Joshua trees. Off to the west the stream makes sporadic showings, with cottonwoods decorating the streamside. Then the moisture goes underground again.

To the right is the Bird Spring Canyon road and it, too, reaches across the lower Sierra Nevada to Highway 14.

There are a number of ranches along this run of foothills—most of them abandoned. An ancient adobe building stands near the road at one point and around it are old soldered tin cans and bits of broken purple glass, indicating a certain antiquity.

The paved road starts its descent through the South Fork Valley toward Weldon. Corn and other grains have been harvested here.

Early in the winter monumental flocks of blackbirds flew up as we drove past, darkening the sky, then wheeling and coming back to light again in the stubble. Along the hills to the west furrowers had been at work, leaving geometric patterns in the land that will be green by early spring with new grains and grasses.

Ahead, on the hill, is the old Weldon tungsten mill, quiet now but once a busy producer.

In early days, according to Bailey, Weldon was an Indian village with the name of Tush-pan. Bailey claims that in 1863, during the Civil War, a temporary U. S. Army outpost known as Camp Leonard was situated here.

Weldon is named for a pioneer area cattleman. An old slaughter house and parts of a flour mill mark the community's link with the past.

The joy of this desert-foothill byway is the fact that it is so easy to drive. Even though you are off pavement for a number of miles there are no problems.

Second, the country is largely unspoiled. Abandoned cabins are here or there, but even the presence of the Windy Acres development on the hillside just south of Weldon does not take away the charm of the rural country.

There are not many places in southern California where you can drive from highway to highway for almost fifty miles without a gas station or curio outpost. It is most refreshing.

The Piute Mountains—if fair weather allows you to drive to old Claraville and the Lander Meadows-French Meadows region—are even more unspoiled.

And if you could bottle that Piute Mountain air and bring it home to sell, you would never have to worry about social security.

VIII

FROM THE BEACH TO THE MOUNTAINS

Fun to explore—any time of the year
Length of exploration—can be driven in a day

SOUTHERN CALIFORNIA's surf-tamped beaches and shattered granite mountains lie within easy vision of one another. Yet there are few byways with the avowed purpose of connecting the two.

State Highway 39 accomplishes this. It is footed in the Pacific Ocean at Huntington Beach and runs like a crooked stick northward, enters the San Gabriel Mountains at Azusa, and climbs then to Crystal Lake, one of the Angeles National Forest's most attractive recreation areas.

Besides connecting those two popular playground areas, Highway 39 provides a look at the classically typical southern California. For along its run are new housing developments where the luxury homes rise from ground that held orange trees so recently that the blossoms can almost still be breathed. Here, too, are orange groves, a vanishing sight in the area. And almost next door to this trademark of an earlier southern California, is a trademark of a newer southern California, miles of oil fields, fenced hill plots where stubby mechanical devices siphon up the black crude and pump it into tanks where gauges have been said to measure the daily flow in dollars instead of gallons.

Here is a sampling of the oddball veneer of the southern California landscape that delights and puzzles the visitor. Pizza parlors, a street corner art gallery, pet cemetery, oil tanks painted pastel, hitch-hiking five-foot-tall boys accompanied by their seven-foot surfboards, a geometric patch of strawberries sewn in a field-sized canvas of plastic which keeps down the weeds.

87

Highway 39 explores it all as it runs from the pulse of surf to the exhalation of mountain winds: real estate offices, discount stores, a hill out of Monet—bright with eucalyptus trees, their pale bark glowing in afternoon sunlight.

As you move north, across Stanton and Buena Park and the City of Industry and La Puente, ahead, like a bright signal, bulks the peak of Old Baldy. Even by spring it can be snow-dusted and in pronounced contrast to the dark blue sky over the San Gabriels.

Let us start, then, at Huntington Beach and drive the byway north into the mountains. If we are slowed, or stopped, by sights or spectaculars along the way and the exploration takes a second day, it is still a worthy adventure. It is not well to measure byway explorations by hours, but rather by the pleasures totaled at the end of the route.

By early morning Huntington Beach is a quieter place. The surfer's supply stores are not yet open and the hamburger shops along the beach front avenue are not engaged in their deep-fry alchemy. But the surfers are here early, laboriously carrying their fiberglassed boards from car to water's edge. If the water and air is cold these adventurers may be outfitted in rubber wet suits, but the surfer is a person apart. He subscribes to few convential moods and discomforts. The surf at Huntington Beach is exceptional and access is simple. Early morning finds the fraternity here; some with their boards stacked on the beach, talking and smoking; some paddling out beyond the end of the long pier; some resting out there in the calm water beyond the break of the big waves; and a few riding the waves in that fantastic ballet.

A gull's eye view of this activity can be had from the Huntington Beach Pier which walks on cemented legs for several hundred feet out into deep water. From the pier it is easy to hang over the edge of the rail and watch the surfers.

Also rail-draped early in the morning are The Faithful: the pier

The long pier at Huntington Beach offers several pleasures: fishing, surf-watching, or just plain dozing in the sun

The general store at Knott's Berry Farm

fishermen who come in search of perch and halibut and the sunny —or foggy—solitude and serenity that pier fishing affords. You'll find the veterans here outfitted with folding stools, a suitcase-sized tackle box, some sort of a grapel to fish up clusters of mussels that grow on the pier pilings (for mussels make excellent bait) and a lunch or thermos. The Faithful here come in all sizes, all ages, either sex. Costumes are casual and conversation is rarely prolonged. These folks come to fish, and pier fishing carries with it a langauge of studied silence, of meditation, of a special peace.

As the day warms here the State Beach, just to the south of the pier, becomes active.

Huntington State Beach opened in May of 1950. Two miles long, Huntington State Beach stretches from State Highway 39 south to the mouth of the Santa Ana River. There are approximately seventy-eight acres in the parcel.

The beach here is used in a monumental way. There are twelve parking lots for this crowd, which materializes mainly in the summer months. There are parking places for 1550 cars, ten comfort stations, 550 fire rings, five food concession buildings and trailers that rent beach equipment.

Why do people come to Huntington State Beach? At times, by night, they come to catch grunion. They come to surf. Bird watchers come here to keep an eye on the shore birds: the gulls, the brown pelicans, the western willets, and the least tern. (From April until June the tern nests here and will do battle to preserve its clutch of eggs. But since the nest is only a depression in the sand, and since the eggs are sand colored, many nestlings are destroyed by strand pedestrians.)

From here the sea lion, the porpoise and even the gray whale can be seen off shore. Surf fishing occupies many visitors' hours here, and at minus tide Pismo clams can be found.

North of the State Beach, and along the Pacific Coast Highway,

Beasts of the California Alligator Farm

is a great ugly steam plant which hulks with a pair of unsightly stacks to break the otherwise pleasant horizon along the flat beach-line.

It is here, at the Pacific Coast Highway, that State Highway 39 starts its run north. It is called Beach Boulevard.

At first the country it travels through is unimpressive. There is building going on here, oceanside subdivisions and tract apartments. But the pace of big business is not yet much in evidence.

The small community of Midway City is passed. Here the Garden Grove Freeway makes its mark on its way to join the San Diego Freeway with the Newport Freeway.

Garden Grove, Stanton, then the Buena Park-Anaheim area is entered. The Highway is busy with business now: here are giant supermarkets, discount houses, ornate hamburger stands.

Knott's Berry Farm and Ghost Town is an enormous private recreation complex that was born of a plot of youngberry vines planted here by Walter Knott in the 1920s. Knott practiced a hard-nosed, fair-play kind of business from the start. He exported berry plants. If you ordered 100 vines and only 94 of them lived, you wrote Knott and he sent you six more plants. No questions.

Extensive berry farms all over California came into being from the plants sold by Knott in Buena Park.

In the depression years Knott built a stand and started selling hot rolls, pies and berry jam. In 1934 his wife, Cordelia, already busy making berry pies, added chicken dinners. Business boomed from that day and never stopped booming. To entertain the people who stood in line to wait for his chicken dinners, Knott built a little 1849-style ghost town. That, too, has grown fantastically. Today four million visitors come to see the Ghost Town and to eat fried chicken and berry pie. Knott no longer sells berry plants. All his farm's spare room has gone over to parking lots.

Across the street from Knott's Berry Farm, to the north of

The Movieland Wax Museum

La Palma, is the California Alligator Farm, transplanted in 1953 from its old location at Lincoln Park. Here hundreds of great scaled alligators, crocodiles, caiman snooze in heated pools. In other tanks are various other creatures that pass for alligators. Turtles and tortoises are on display. In enclosed pens are snakes— one great block of these is devoted to poisonous snakes. Huge boas, water snakes, harmless racers and garden snakes are on display along with mambas, cobras, vipers, rattlesnakes. A thoroughly fascinating display where, at regular intervals, a guided tour with an informative lecture is given.

On up the street a block or so, is the newer Movieland Wax Museum.

More than $1,000,000 went into the construction of the displays, which opened in 1962. Wax models of famous motion picture stars stand in familiar scenes—sometimes from movies that made them famous, sometimes in authentic behind-the-footlight settings. On hand are models of the greats, living and dead, such as Bela Lugosi as Dracula, Lon Chaney as The Phantom of the Opera, Rudolph Valentino, Norma Shearer, Ginger Rogers, Fred Astaire, Will Rogers, Jean Harlow, Wallace Beery and Clark Gable.

Now our byway ducks under the busy Santa Ana Freeway, bends slightly to the east and passes the Los Coyotes Hills area.

An area of the hill country now is fenced from the public and behind the chain link oil pumps duck and bob busily sluicing up oil from the deposits that are under title of Standard Oil.

At the edge of East Whittier and La Habra, Beach Boulevard ends; the state highway signs take the motorist onto a stretch of Whittier Boulevard briefly for a short distance to the east, then the highway heads north again along Hacienda Boulevard.

This is the region of the vanishing orange groves. There are still many here, particularly on the south side of the hills. But as the

94

Eucalypti shade the hills near La Habra

summit is gained and the road drops from attractive eucalyptus shaded hills terraced by cattle to the north, the orange groves are being taken out even now to make room for a great assortment of homes in exclusive subdivisions.

And always, to the north, burns the bright beacon of Old Baldy.

Through Hacienda Heights, Industry, La Puente, the road name changes to Glendora Boulevard. There are schools and poodle parlors, country clubs and gun shops, billboards and grass-grown empty lots—but fewer of the latter each month.

There is a tricky maneuver as the State Highway twists to the east, crosses under the San Bernardino Freeway, and runs north again as Azusa Avenue.

West Covina, Covina, Azusa, are passed through, and the State Highway 39 is still spotted with businesses. North of Azusa our by-way becomes the San Gabriel Canyon Road.

It enters the great cleft in the purple-green San Gabriel Mountains along a historic watercourse.

A few miles upcanyon we come to Morris Dam, a cement structure built by the City of Pasadena in 1932-1934. The structure, 756 feet wide at the top, and 245 feet high, is designed to hold back 42,000-acre-feet of water.

The dam, the damsite and the lake have been used since 1943 by the U. S. Navy for testing underwater missiles and torpedoes. That great erector-set-looking structure you'll see as you drive by —the site is open to the public usually only on Armed Forces Day —is a variable-angle torpedo launcher.

On upstream further is another dam. This one is earth and stone instead of concrete. The structure is labeled San Gabriel Dam Number 1 and the scars where the fill for the dam came down off the eastern hills are plainly seen.

There is a bridge and a side road to the east here into the East Fork country, site of a last-century gold strike. We continue north,

At the end of the byway, up near Angeles Crest, is peaceful Crystal Lake

pass the road into the West Fork and come to the first of several Forest Service picnic and camping sites.

Coldbrook is the first of these; there are other sites along the river where picnicking is allowed. Camping is permitted only in specified campgrounds.

Sections of the highway here, a bit at a time, are being widened. In time the entire run of the canyon road from Azusa to Crystal Lake will be thus improved. Some old-timers liked it best the way it was—narrow and winding.

There is the business of climbing now, and the road makes a series of looping switchbacks. Here is the private resort—open to the public—of Falling Springs. In an ideal setting, with running water and green, green foliage everywhere, a visit to or a stay at Falling Springs can be an impressive mountain experience.

The Crystal Lake Recreation Area is built around two features —the small spot of water here known as Crystal Lake, and the much larger and much more attractive Forest Service Campground.

There is a bait shop, boat rental, snack bar, etc., at the lake, which is most pleasant when viewed through the sheltering trees. Still for all its shortcomings of sylvan beauty, it attracts hundreds each year for fishing. By late summer algae rides on the surface of the lake and the shore is dusty. But in a lake-shy area, it is a place to row a boat and to fish.

The Angeles National Forest has spent a good deal of money and effort in making the Crystal Lake Campground one of the finest. There is a store here, and most of the conveniences. Youth groups make this their hideout on almost all campable weekends, but there is still room for casual picnickers and overnight campers who enjoy the smell of pinewood smoke in the mountains and relish the feel of the pine-doctored wind.

From Crystal Lake a brief avenue, called by Forest Service people "the Crystal Lake Spur," finishes the run of State Highway 39. This colorful byway ends at Islip Saddle, the junction of State Highway 39 and State Highway 2—the Angeles Crest Highway.

Here the elevation is close to 7,000 feet; pine trees stand against the sky; big-horn sheep have been seen on all the nearby promontories, but they are shy and spotting one takes the patience of an experienced naturalist. Just to the west is the San Gabriel Wilderness.

Our byway has dramatized some of the best that southern California has to offer in a way that can be enjoyed and appreciated by motorists new and old to the region.

Ask a surfer: there is no place quite like Huntington Beach.

Ask a mountaineer: there is no place just the same as Crystal Lake an Mt. Islip and Little Jimmy Springs and the deeps of Bear Canyon.

The crooked stick of the road that connects these two uncommon places does its job well.

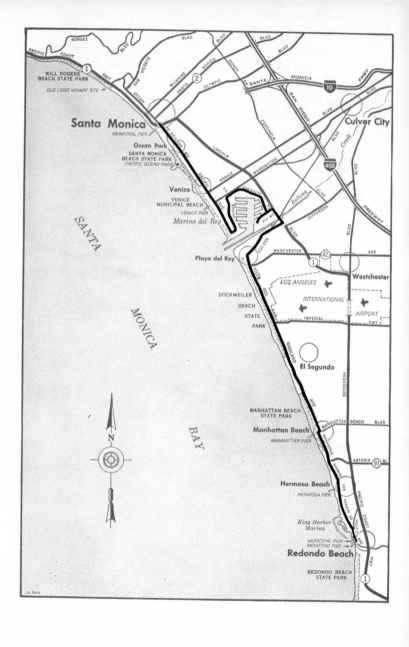

IX ALONG THE PIERS OF SANTA MONICA BAY

Fun to explore—any time of the year
Length of exploration—can be driven in a day

ONE DAY IN 1959 the white sea bass hit the Santa Monica Municipal Pier like a finny flood. They roiled in the surf and struck at almost anything that was offered. Two hundred of them were caught in a single afternoon and these ranged from fifteen to forty-two pounds. The run continued for a week, the bass coming in during daylight and after dark. The railings of the pier were lined with fishermen.

That same year, according to veteran Santa Monica newspaperman and pier expert Bill Beebe, the barracuda ran at Santa Monica. Frantic fishermen were catching them off the pier and in the surf. One desperate angler, unable to buy a lure at the stampeded tackle shop, fashioned one out of a beer can opener, fished happily in the surf, giving away the barracuda as fast as he caught them.

This angler had a fever, old-timers will point out. As a rule the Santa Monica Pier is not a feverish place. It is a venerable and quiet site. The pier is a half century old and shows it. The veterans who fish here regularly can recall with a kind of pleasure the music that emanated from a vanished ballroom and the muted clatter of a roller coaster that arched nearby.

Pier fishing along Santa Monica Bay is strongly steeped in a sort of mood, and the mood usually is peaceful. There are a handful of the fine piers—old and new—between Santa Monica and Redondo Beach where the gentle sport is offered. Certainly there are currents of excitement that run in the salty stream here. Surfers ply

101

*At private piers such as this one, it is necessary to have a
fishing license, not required at public municipal piers*

the water away from the piers. Boat races are held within and outside the breakwaters. One mad day a series of waterspouts was seen marching on the Santa Monica Pier. A few moments later it rained anchovies on the beach. But mainly it is peaceful along this waterfront from Santa Monica to Redondo.

The first pier in the Santa Monica area dates back to the era of dispute about the location of a harbor for the city of Los Angeles. Nevada's Senator John P. Jones held that Santa Monica was the likeliest spot and built a pier there in 1875. His railroad into the city was called the Los Angeles and Independence—he hoped to drive the line out through the Cajon Pass and then up into the Owens Valley.

But the Los Angeles and Independence got as far from Santa Monica as Los Angeles and struck the shoal of poor financing. The Southern Pacific acquired the line, tore down the original pier.

Then they built a grander version. In 1891-92 the Long Wharf was constructed near the mouth of Santa Monica canyon; its length was 4,700 feet. The seaside cliffs were tunneled and cut and a railroad line ran out to and on the 130-foot-wide structure. At the end of the Long Wharf was a depot and dining room; buoys were anchored so that ships could tie up and unload at the railhead hanging over six and one-half fathoms of water. The pleasure pier attracted fishermen from its opening.

The Southern Pacific's gamble that Santa Monica would be the site of the Los Angeles harbor was lost, and in 1912 the Long Wharf was torn down. Enough of the ruins of the pier remain underwater to make the site a good fishing spot.

In 1909 the Municipal Pier was opened in Santa Monica and the city celebrated. There are a few old hands around who fished off the pier that day and who are still wetting a line in Santa Monica Bay. Each pier has its regulars, and the Santa Monica structure is no exception. This is home during the daylight hours

New piers like the one at Venice
   are built of concrete

for about a dozen dedicated fisherfolk who come—as a rule—six days a week. Sunday, some of them explain, is the Sabbath, not good for fishing. They arrive early, usually between seven and eight, armed with tackle box, poles, bucket and burlap bags.

When a piling is being pulled they congregate, because they know that here can be found the best mussels and worms for bait. They all try for pile perch, which they consider good eating, and often land them up to a pound in size. Most of the tomcod caught goes to Tomcod Mary who has a market for it somewhere, and the rest of the catch, depending on luck and whim of the fishing deities, is made up of herring, perch and corbina, halibut and mackerel, sand sharks and skates, even bonita and yellowtail.

These regulars insist there is more than a sport here. There is even more than the salt-water fellowship. Offered is a kind of medicine of sun and fresh air and working breezes; offered is a kind of peace in the communion with nature.

Others, following the regulars in hours and determination, come to these piers. Some come only to fish and go home angry if they are empty-handed. But many more come because it is soul-knitting to sit in the fog or sunshine and watch the march of the small waves upon the beach.

Here at Santa Monica Municipal Pier, and at all public piers, no fishing license is required to fish. At piers where there is a charge, a license is required. The Santa Monica Pier is open daily and open and patrolled all night. There are rowboat rentals here and a boat hoist.

Adjacent to the pier is a row of fish markets and cafes, the usual trappings of a pier area. Here is an old organ-inspired merry-go-round. The carousel is housed on the ground floor of an apartment building and a sign outside reads:

"The only apartment house in the world that has a merry-go-round and an organ. In the morning the guests awake to the tunes

105

On summer weekends the Monstad Pier in Redondo Beach
supports a forest of fishing poles

of the organ and all day they go about their duties with music in their ears. When they are ready to go to bed the music helps put them to sleep. People come from all parts of the world to rent apartments in this building . . ."

Pointing south from Santa Monica Pier it is possible to follow lesser byways during some of the passage. First we follow Ocean Boulevard, then Neilson Way is gained. Here is a section of the Santa Monica Beach State Park, perhaps one of the most heavily used beaches on the Bay.

South now on Neilson Way, past Pacific Ocean Park, our byway leads into that portion of Los Angeles known as Venice—Venice of the wondrous canals.

This is Pacific Avenue now, but it is possible to edge down toward the ocean and gain the historic, one-way narrow Speedway.

The beach along here is famous and is serviced by a tram.

The Speedway, which is no longer fast, but interrupted by dozens of stop signs, ends at Westminster Avenue and from here it is necessary to get back on Pacific Avenue. The old Venice Pavilion is passed and at the foot of Washington Street is the new Venice Pier.

Opened in 1965, the Venice Pier was built with matching funds from the state's Wildlife Conservation Board and the City of Los Angeles. It is 1,310 feet long and 16 feet wide, built of concrete. There is an open fishing circle of 120-foot diameter at the seaward end, as well as individual fishing stations, benches and lights at 84-foot intervals along the pier's slender run. It is a $900,000 structure. Already the pier has attracted its share of regulars who find that, while the fishing is not yet the best, the wind and the sunshine are unspoiled by the pier's newness.

Pacific Avenue runs on south, past some of the decayed canal bridges that once made Venice famous, ends at the mouth of the Marina del Rey. There is no bridge across the channel; it is neces-

What does a sign mean to a small boy who has just had his first nibble of the day?

sary to backtrack. Take northward-running Via Marina to skirt this fantastic apartment-decorated small-boat anchorage. By following Via Marina, Admiralty Way and then east a short distance on Fiji Way, it is possible to pick up Lincoln Boulevard, then Jefferson Boulevard back to the beaches south of the Marina's mouth.

Here we follow Vista Del Mar through Playa Del Rey. The Dockweiler Beach State Park stands here, complete with fire rings. Never quite as crowded as some of the Bay's other beaches, Dockweiler offers 650 picnic sites.

The big structures along the beach here are the Hyperion Treatment Plant and the Scattergood Steam Plant. At El Segundo the long oil pier is closed to public fishing.

Vista Del Mar Boulevard becomes Highland Avenue as you enter Manhattan Beach. At the foot of Manhattan Beach Boulevard is the Manhattan Pier.

Originally a municipal operation, the beach and pier were deeded to the state in 1946 and are now operated by the County of Los Angeles.

The first pier at Manhattan, built in 1902, was distinguished by the fact that it housed a wave motion machine which was supposed to have tapped the sea's swell to generate power.

A longer, 1,000-footer, was completed in 1923, but not until a handful of bond issues was passed and the city had a legal wrestling match with the contractor. At one juncture the contractor threatened to tear down all that he had built. A picket line of impassioned citizens prevented this calamity.

Material for the Manhattan Pier was brought in by boat and lighter, and mules tugged the pilings and plankings around in the sand.

The pier today is part of the Manhattan Beach State Park.

Hermosa Beach, reached via Hermosa Avenue, has the newest of the municipal piers facing Santa Monica Bay. Opened in 1965, the Hermosa Pier, like its Venice counterpart, was built with matching funds offered by the State Wildlife Conservation Board and the city. It cost $600,000.

The fishing pier, made of concrete, is 1,168 feet long, 20 wide and has a 50- by 68-foot platform at its terminus. Here there is a tackle shop, a snack bar, rest rooms, and a boat landing.

There are 1,850 feet of rail space for fishermen and on weekends they are apt to be crowded. There are eleven benches and four drinking fountains. Beyond the pier a $23,000 artificial reef is planned.

Hermosa Avenue becomes Harbor Drive and Redondo Beach is reached. The luxurious King Harbor Marina is passed and at the center of Redondo Beach is the Monstad Pier-Municipal Pier complex. Here there are water taxis running out to fishing barges, harbor cruises, pier fishing, pier dining; a busy, busy place.

There is a Fisherman's Wharf with fish markets and fashionable seafood restaurants. On the Monstad Pier is the sport fishing base for the sport fishing boats. Water taxis run from the pier every half hour to the five fishing barges anchored in this end of the Bay. One of these barges is is the old paddlewheeler from San Francisco Bay, the *Sacramento,* another is an old Navy cargo ship.

Two excursion boats, the *Lonie* and the *Voyager,* offer half-hour cruises of the harbor. A large two-decked parking lot has been built adjacent to the Fisherman's Wharf but there always seems to be a parking problem, so popular is the facility.

Pier fishing here tends a little toward the frantic at times. Fishermen may stand shoulder to shoulder along the railing of the Monstad. Bait and tackle are available nearby and if you miss catching a yellowtail or a bonita, take home a couple of pounds of smoked salmon from one of the open-fronted fish markets instead.

Pier fishing is one of the most healthful sports offered to southern Californians. Retired folks, those who have led an active life but who have been ordered to slow down, find this sport satisfying in all ways.

The State Department of Fish and Game reports that in an area from Point Conception to the Mexican border, fishermen put in 5.1 million man hours on pier and jetty fishing in a year's time. And they caught 1.86 million fish.

For the curious, the most common fish of forty-nine species in their haul were queen perch (also known locally as herring), white croaker (otherwise known as tomcod), walleyed surf perch, bonita and shiner perch. Among the exotic hooked were bonefish and frigate mackerel.

Our byway has followed a peaceful path along Santa Monica Bay and has paused here and there at the fishing piers. There is plenty to recommend pier exploring. Artists like to take sketch pad and crayon along, the photographer finds many oblivious human subjects to catch at peace or in action. If you wish to join the fraternity, there is always room for one more fisherman along the rail.

Even when the wild wind is keening in off the Pacific and the little surf has piled high and gray, there is a quiet excitement in walking the spray-blown piers. You'll still find the regulars here: Tomcod Mary and Mackerel Benny will have their favorite spot along the railing. The herring or the pile perch will be biting and the problems of the world can wait.

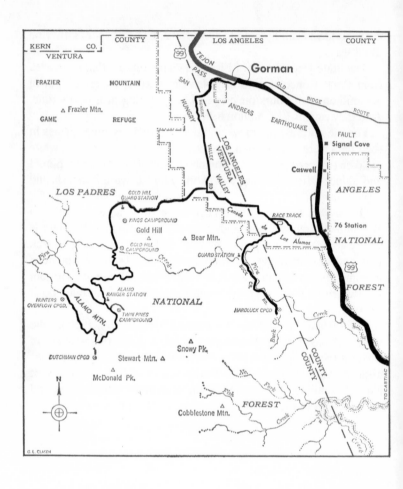

X UP ONTO
ALAMO MOUNTAIN

Fun to explore—closed in the winter
Road can be rough in the early spring
Length of exploration—can be driven in a day

ONE OF THE most persistent of the vanished mine legends of
southern California concerns the Los Padres Mine. It is associated
with various missions: San Fernando, San Buenaventura, and
Santa Barbara.

In some accounts it is a gold mine that is lost. In at least one it
is an enormously rich silver mine.

The locale of the lost mine ranges from the Mill Creek area of
the Angeles National Forest to the tributaries of Piru Creek
around Alamo Mountain in Ventura County's Los Padres National
Forest.

Many old-timers favor the region bordering the Ridge Route,
claim that it is the most likely for the Los Padres lode, that it was
first discovered by the padres of Santa Barbara.

Old stories tell of days, before secularization, when there were
"stacks of buillion lying around" in the mission buildings. Where
did it come from? Some claim the gravel deposits along Piru
Creek.

More recent history records that there was much gold activity
in this area. Around 1875 gold claims were being worked northeast of Alamo Mountain. Records of the California Division of
Mines tell of activity in the Piru District prior to 1894.

Place names bear out the early mining activity. Here is sprawling Gold Hill, with both a ranger station and a campground carrying the place name.

113

Perhaps somewhere in the broken country, along Piru Creek, carefully hidden, is the old mine of the padres, waiting for an act of nature to reveal its presence.

This whole region (with one exception) has few visitors. It is less than two hours drive from Los Angeles, it offers, in season, snow, running streams, cool mountain air, wildflowers, and yet the average weekend will find not more than a handful of visitors here. Even by deep summer, the summit of Alamo Mountain, 7,455 feet —above the heat and smog of southern California—can be a lonesome spot.

The one exception is the first weekend of early deer season. On this weekend the region attracts hunters in incredible numbers. Last year 6,000 were counted on Alamo Mountain on a Saturday and Sunday. The weekend before the count was less than a dozen.

There are a number of reasons to visit Alamo Mountain. The loneliness is only one of its charms. Add to this the cool summer air, pine scented and brightened with small breezes that move in from the ocean. The road that explores Alamo Mountain is a loop drive with some of the most exciting vistas in southern California.

The whole region of upper Ventura County and lower Kern County is a scenic delight. All the peaks in the area have great charm. Frazier Mountain, Mount Pinos, Abel Mountain, Sawmill Mountain, Cobblestone Mountain, McDonald Peak, are little known and seldom visited, nevertheless.

Getting to Alamo Mountain is not simple. It requires finding a tricky turnoff from the Ridge Route (U. S. Highway 99). North of Castaic some twenty miles is a gas station-restaurant with a 76 sign. (If you get as far as the site of abandoned Signal Cove you have gone too far.) North of the 76 station, one-quarter of a mile —our odometer showed three-tenths of a mile—there is a dirt road turning off the highway to the west. It will still be there after the eight-laned freeway is completed in the area.

At the junction of Buck Creek and Piru Creek there is a strange outcropping of pitted rock

Follow this as it crosses private property, drops south even with 76 station again, passes a little reservoir, and finally heads west. A small race track is passed. This is a corridor through private land maintained by the Forest Service. On the map the area is called Cañada de Los Alamos. About three miles from its beginning is a road fork. Alamo Mountain lies along the right hand fork, but briefly we'll take a side trip down a length of Piru Creek. It runs down to Buck Creek and is called the Buck Creek Road.

The left hand road gains a promontory, heads down a hill that would not offer a comfortable passage for any vehicle pulling a trailer, and enters the Los Padres National Forest. Near at hand now is the old corral left behind when the Piru Creek ranger station was torn down.

The road crosses Piru Creek—even by late spring a sizeable stream of water. By summer it may be almost dry, but there could be a trickle in the course. Through some interesting lower country the road moves back to Hardluck Campground, passing, along the way, many stands of cottonwood and willow where Piru Creek has paused and made a sign. In the spring and winter this stretch is stocked with fish. There is a good trail leading out of the canyon reaching southwest toward McDonald Peak and Alamo Mountain.

Back at the road fork we continue to the right, and in three miles come to another road junction. The right hand road this time leads up to Gorman. We will take the left hand course here into the Gold Hill area. The two peaks to the southwest are Bear Mountain, elevation 4,777 feet, and Gold Hill, elevation 4,838 feet.

This is the historic gold mining district of the region. Several mines are shown on maps. A jeep track curves away to the south toward the vanished camp site of old Gold Hill.

The main road curves toward the west and south to the Gold Hill ranger station, manned only in the summer months. A tent station, it serves a large section of this remote area.

From this point the road runs south, reaches a side road which

116

The loop around Alamo Mountain's summit is a peaceful, if winding avenue, marked by Jeffrey and ponderosa pine

runs one mile back into the Kings Campground, and continues south to Piru Creek, another segment of the same watercourse we visited on the Buck Creek Road.

Chances are better here of water in the stream. When we visited it in mid-May there were fishermen, waders and gold dredgers at work. The road fords the stream—in early spring when the water is really deep this is as far as you can go. There is a small campground here. Ahead lies Alamo Mountain.

This road is graded all the way to the top after the winter rains and the snowy runoff of spring. Remember that the road can be a rough and rubbly one if it has not been graded since the winter. A good idea is to check with a Forest Service ranger—you are sure to find one at the Chuchupate Ranger Station just beyond Frazier Park. If the road is rough and rubbly it is better explored in a pickup or jeep.

Through pinyon pine and juniper the road seeks a gentle climbing route to one overlook after another.

Up where Piru Creek joins with Lockwood Creek there is a flat of maybe seventy-five acres. An old settlement once stood here—its name is forgotten even by the oldtimers. The settlers made their living from the gravel golds and at least part of the camp was made up of Chinese. Some old purple bottles have been found at the site, reachable today only by jeep.

Up and up the Alamo Mountain byway climbs. This is the area of a vast fire that swept through the country in 1950. Many of the stands of Jeffrey pine were killed and downed in that blaze. The road, built during a salvage logging operation after the fire, dates back to 1954.

More timber land is gained. Finally the road makes a last climb and reaches the Alamo ranger station, recently renamed the Big Springs station. There is a supply of good cold mountain water here and a large watering trough for the cattle that occasionally graze on the mountain.

*There is farming country in the region north of Alamo
Mountain, on the road back to Gorman*

A short distance up the hill we come to a road fork. This is the beginning and the end of the loop road around the summit of Alamo Mountain.

There are two campgrounds along the loop: Twin Pines, with a half dozen campsites and in the process of being moved to a much larger site; and Dutchman with only a pair of sites.

Less than a half mile from the beginning of the loop trail and southeast of the road fork, an unsigned side road leads east into the Twin Pine Campground.

We followed the loop by driving first toward the north. The area just visited along Piru Creek is visible. The dirt road down past Gold Hill and Kings Campground is in plain view.

As the road curves toward the west the juncture of Piru and Lockwood Creeks comes into view. Here the old mountain community was hidden.

On west then, with the Mutau country appearing beyond the pined ridges. Once, it is said, there was a settlement and a school in the Mutau. It is lonesome country now.

As the road curves toward the south the distant Sespe region shows up. It is here that the nation's only condor sanctuary lies and here are the last few remaining condors in North America—an estimated forty of the birds.

Condors are frequently seen in the area of Alamo Mountain. They call in deer season, looking for slaughtered deer that hunters have not found or have left because they have discovered their kills were illegal spike bucks or does.

A great flatland here along the loop road is turned into a temporary campground for hunters during deer season. It would make an ideal permanent campground—high, cool, flat and shaded.

On south, the road comes to a double fork off to the right. The lesser road is the jeep track that runs down to the Piru Creek-Lockwood Creek meeting and then follows Lockwood Creek—

Here the dirt road to Hardluck Campground crosses Piru Creek.

By spring camping is pleasant along Piru Creek.

traveling in the stream part of the way—to Lockwood Valley. The other road runs down hill to the Dutchman camp site, small, but pleasant.

South, still, and then the road begins to curve toward the east. Off to the south are Stewart Mountain and McDonald Peak.

The fire missed this side of the mountain and the Jeffrey pine and occasional fir are dense. But one of the forest's natural enemies, dwarf mistletoe, has infected the pines here. The parasite is a crippler and a killer and many pines are gnarled and dying because of the infestation. Few link the romantic mistletoe with such grim effects.

At the southernmost point of this loop road a rough side road reaches away toward Stewart Mountain and McDonald Peak. We did not explore it; were told that it was more suitable for jeeps.

East and north now, past the beginning of the trail down into Snowy Peak country designated for trail bikes. Then back to road fork—the end of the loop.

It is a pity that there is no regular access to the very summit of Alamo Mountain (there is a jeep track), even if there were nothing more than a parking area. There should be more trails and certainly more campgrounds. The two campsites—Twin Pines and Dutchman—are not nearly enough.

There is another route back to Highway 99. Return to that road fork north of Gold Hill. Take the northbound track up through Hungry Valley. It is about six miles through some peaceful flatland country, with Frazier Mountain bulking to the west, to the Ridge Route. The entrance is exactly one mile north of Gorman proper. Again, alas, there is no sign.

Thousands of people hurry past Gorman each day, none of them dreaming that there is such country as Alamo Mountain hidden back here.

Such surprises are the principal joys of byway exploration.

122

XI INTO THE TEHACHAPIS

Fun to explore—good anytime of the year
Length of exploration—can be driven in a day

SOUTHERN CALIFORNIA is crossed by a number of transverse mountain ranges and perhaps none of them is embroidered with more history then the westernmost San Gabriel Mountains as they meld with the Tehachapis in the Ridge Route country.

Through this tangle of hills and pines and chaparral the early-day travelers etched a mountain crossing. Here, in a protected fold in the mountains, was one of the Far West's earliest army forts. And as the owners of the land have changed, some unusual beasts have lived here: Arabian horses, Russian wolfhounds, camels and ostriches.

By autumn the route out along the western arm of the San Gabriels and into the Tehachapis is cool and pleasant. At the higher elevations the wind can have a bite to it—but conversely the day can be as balmy as May, sunspeckled under the giant oaks and pines and brushed with a gentler breeze.

This byway exploration starts at Palmdale, at the southern edge of the Antelope Valley, an historic agriculture and railroad community, one that has known the thrum of aerospace industry in recent years.

The new Antelope Valley Freeway now runs northeast from Solemint through Palmdale on its path toward the historic Tehachapi Pass.

Our course west out of Palmdale is known variously along its run: Palmdale Boulevard, then a small section of Avenue Q, fin-

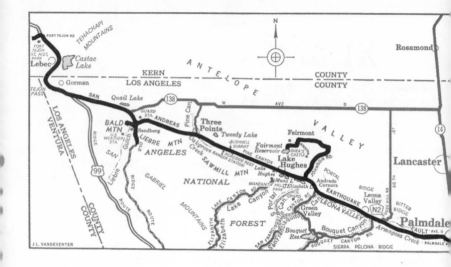

ally Elizabeth Lake. It is the same byway as it travels this fold of the San Gabriels, the course of the infamous San Andreas earthquake fault.

Just west of Palmdale, beyond the fringe of housing, a patch of Joshua trees intrudes. The road winds and curves, slides between the Ritter Ridge on the north and the Sierra Pelona Ridge on the south. At the Forest Service lookout tower on Sierra Pelona Ridge winter winds up to 100 miles an hour have been recorded.

This is dry Amargosa Creek we follow—no relation to the more famous Amargosa River in Death Valley.

The land is fenced and is used mostly for cattle graze. Lonesome windmills—the older ones frozen on their last heading—are silhouetted against the greening hills.

This march of byway is signed route N2, a country road designation.

124

A gnarled oak guards the road between Quail Lake fire station and Highway 138.

There is a junction with the Goode Hill Road and just opposite, on the south side of the highway, a private hunting ranch. A short distance beyond is the junction with the Bouquet Canyon Road leading south through the hills toward Saugus. The canyon takes its name, not from any floral offering, but from the fact that an early settler was a former sailor and his many stories about his ships, *"el buque,"* resulted in the corruption of that into "bouquet."

Our byway now travels through Leona Valley. One version attributes the place name to Miguel Leonis, an early day settler.

Primarily cattle country, there may even be a herd of horses or a string of burros behind barbed wire here.

The junction with the San Francisquito Canyon Road is here called Andrade Corners. This canyon reaches south into some of the most interesting country in this arm of the San Gabriels. South of the community of Green Valley the road is still unpaved and narrow, but the side canyon Forest Service campground of South Portal is one of the joys of the area.

A short distance west of the San Francisquito Canyon turnoff is Johnson Road, the old Munz Canyon road, heading north. This is the route of the old Los Angeles to Willow Springs stageline.

North on Johnson Road four and a half miles and west then four miles brings the explorer to the site of old Fairmont. Via a zigzag course—south, then west, then south—is the historic Fairmont Reservoir, a water depository for the Los Angeles Aqueduct. A couple of miles to the east, on the same dirt road that leads to the reservoir access, takes the explorer to the fenced expanse that holds mysterious Shea's Castle, a storied monument hulking against the north slope of Portal Ridge. Even the locked gate is a curiosity.

Back on N2, close at hand, is Elizabeth Lake, a sink along the San Andreas Fault. By winter the water depth is a sometimes thing.

An old windmill stands frozen on its last heading in this foothill country.

If the rains have been steady the lake can be sizeable. It will be dotted with water birds.

Here is the new Lake Elizabeth Ranch and Golf Club—a private venture. Beyond the Angeles National Forest entrance sign is the resort of Munz Lake, now called Manzanita Hills Park, with camping, picnicking and fishing. Then we pass the small community of Lake Hughes with the lake badly in need of water.

There is a turnoff to the south down Elizabeth Lake Canyon— the road here is signed the Lake Hughes Road. This canyon route, paralleling Bouquet and San Francisquito, comes out of the mountains at Castaic. It passes the pleasant campground at Cottonwood and eventually it will meet the new Castaic Lake recreation area created by Feather River water.

It is Pine Canyon that Highway N2 follows to the west of Lake Hughes and pines do begin to appear. On this woodsy-chaparral stretch of highway the county of Los Angeles has fashioned an attractive Pine Canyon Roadside Rest. Here the traveler will find picnic tables and stoves, rest rooms and water. Just beyond is the Pine Canyon ranger station of the Angeles National Forest. Ask here about road conditions if you want to drive up the unpaved route onto Sawmill Mountain. The turnoff is just beyond.

Off to the right of Bushnell Summit, elevation 5,000 feet, is the private road back to Tweedy Lake with a gaggle of cabins. On the left is a mountain lodge offering camping, swimming, trailer spaces.

Oakgrove Creek is followed to Three Points, a junction with a three-mile stretch of road running north to State Highway 138. We continue west, climbing again, passing giant oaks and buckeye on a road narrow, winding, climbing, but always fun to pursue.

At the Quail Lake Guard Station (strangely named for it is more than three miles to Quail Lake) we come to the end of this avenue and a junction with the old Ridge Route.

This is the grandfather of all the Ridge Routes—and, as you will find out on this trip, there is still another new one in the works. Follow south for a while. That strange wooden roadside railing you see in sections here dates back to the 1920s when this was the main avenue between Los Angeles and the San Joaquin Valley. Unpainted for thirty years, the old wooden railing has stood the rigors of time surprisingly well.

The stone wall that stands on the right side of the road is all that is left of old Sandberg's, a resort dating back to the early Ridge Route days. It burned about 1964—an isolated outpost but the only building then left along the old Ridge. A short distance farther south is the gate onto the "unmaintained" portion of the old Ridge Route. If you have the desire to drive the span—it is some twenty-five miles long and comes out at Castaic—don't be frightened. It is a perfectly fine mountain road, rough and narrow in places but never scary nor dangerous. Several old cement foundations indicate some of the old resorts and gas stations that once stood along this busy road.

Our byway adventure backtracks now to the junction of N2 and the old Ridge Route. Off to the left—to the west—is a paved road leading to the top of Bald Mountain and the U.S. Government weather station there. Just a few yards along this road is the unpaved turnoff down into Liebre Gulch. Better leave this side road to jeeps and more rugged exploring vehicles, although it is fascinating country.

North two and a half miles brings us to the junction of State Highway 138. This is Kinsey Ranch country and soon you'll pass the impressive colonial headquarters house of the ranch. Quail Lake, another earthquake fault depression, is off to the right, and following that fault line we run northwest to a junction with U.S. Highway 99, the present Ridge Route. You'll see plenty of evidence just before you get to Gorman of the *newest* Ridge Route, a great eight-laned freeway that is cutting the miles and the pain from driving over these storied mountains.

The mountain community of Gorman is now bypassed by the freeway, and the Tejon Pass Summit has been cut down. Remember when the signs here used to read, "No, the wind never blew like this before?"

Lebec is passed—the doomed hotel fading more each year. Off to the right is the white scar of Castaic Lake.

The turnoff from the freeway onto the Fort Tejon road is plainly marked, and a new parking area has been provided at the entrance. There is a small museum and park headquarters at Fort Tejon State Historic Park, and what a fat book of history this canyon off Grapevine Creek holds.

It was here, originally, that the Indians lived, grew fat on the plentiful game and acorn crop. A Mexican land grant gave the property to Ignacio del Valle. He called the grant Tejon, the Spanish-Indian word for badger.

It was in 1852 that Edward F. Beale arrived. In November that year he was appointed Commissioner of Indian Affairs in California and Nevada. One of his first duties was to establish the San Sebastian Reservation, in the flatland of the San Joaquin Valley just north of Grapevine. Beale suggested at that time the establishment of a military post in the area. The mountain site had wood and water, was on the main traveled route from Los Angeles north, would be situated in a position to watch for horse and cattle thieves.

In the brochure on the historical landmark, the State Division of Beaches and Parks quotes an old source in its description of the site:

"The post of Tejon is on a little plain, entirely surrounded by high mountains, beautifully situated in a grove of old oaks. . . . On the plains and mountain sides, Mother Nature has excelled herself

130

Fairmont Reservoir catches the flow of water from Owens Valley.

. . . the air is bracing and exhilarating and inspiring. An oasis in the desert where all is freshness and life."

A dramatic pronouncement, if not entirely accurate. It is not a desert here, the elevation is 3,200 feet and Grapevine Creek usually has water in it.

The government took heed of Beale's suggestion, started work on the fort on June 23, 1854. At the end of the month a detachment of Company A, First Dragoons, under the command of Lieutenant Thomas A. Castor, moved onto the site. Fort Tejon, in time, became the regimental headquarters for the First Dragoons.

Soldiers from Tejon ranged great distances on their military business. Troubles in Owens Valley were handled, troops were sent to Santa Barbara, others trekked to the Colorado River, served on escorts to Salt Lake City.

In 1858 the Butterfield Overland Mail made a regular stop here. Fort Tejon spread across many acres at its peak and Harris Newmark operated a store here.

In 1864 the post was abandoned, the land then was part of General Beale's rancho. Beale's camel corps was stationed at the site briefly during the 1850s.

The old fort buildings were used as residences, sheds and stables. Most of them, built of adobe, eroded away. In 1939 the first five-acre deed was accepted by the state of California from the Tejon Ranch—the beginning of the State Historic Park. In 1949 restoration of the post began. In 1954 an additional 200 acres were purchased by the state. Only the barracks (not now open to the public), quarters for officers and orderlies (which are open to the public) still stand here now. There are several ruins in the area that will, someday, be the foundations for restorations. Personnel at the site have located three old fort dumps which should provide archaeologists with a bonanza.

Within the grounds is the Peter Lebeck tree. It was here in 1837 that a French adventurer by the name of Peter Lebeck was killed by a bear, possibly a grizzly. He was buried under a nearby oak, but no one has ever determined for sure, just who Lebeck was. At the time of his death his friends, however, carved an epitaph on the old tree and the scar still shows. A curve of oak bark, showing the words, is on display in the small museum at Fort Tejon.

The oaks are enormous around the ghost-trodden parade ground of Fort Tejon. Cattails and wild celery grow along Grapevine Creek and the swift signature of the red-tailed hawk can often be noted in the mountain sky.

All the way from desert-born Palmdale through pastoral Leona Valley into conifer-posted Pine Canyon the journey is one of little traffic and peaceful vistas. There is momentary madness along those few miles of freeway as the Ridge Route thunders from Gorman to the Grapevine, but at the state park the setting is again one of serenity.

The Tehachapis and that westward reaching arm of the San Gabriels provide some of the best there is in the history-dotted mountain country of southern California.

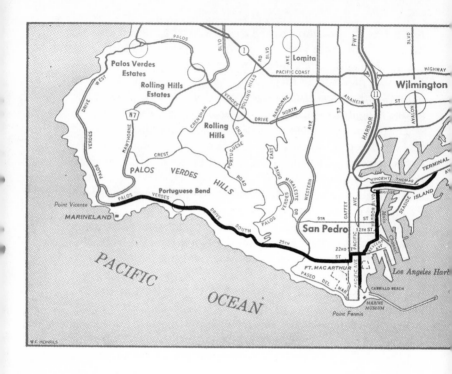

134

XII

FROM MARINELAND
TO TERMINAL ISLAND

Fun to explore—any time of the year
Length of exploration—can be driven in a day

From the top of the spectacular new Sky Tower at Marineland of the Pacific at Palos Verdes you can see up the coast as far as Point Dume, where the low cliffs of the headland shine brightly in the afternoon sun.

To the south, on a summer night, after the wind has scoured away the fog and smog and haze, are the twinkling lights of Newport and Balboa.

Catalina is only twenty-two miles away. But more remote Santa Barbara Island is also spotted at times, riding in the mist of the offshore Pacific swell.

Seeing for miles and miles is what you can do best from the Sky Tower—and it is the reason why the Marineland people added it.

Pictures of a similar tower on the shores of Lake Geneva in Switzerland prompted William F. Monohan, Marineland executive, to give the go-ahead for the spire's construction by a Swiss firm.

The Sky Tower, which stands at the beginning of our byway exploration, is unusual for many reasons. One of these is its unorthodox construction. The elevator of the Sky Tower, a two-tiered affair—each tier holding thirty persons—rides up around the exterior of the Tower. The elevator is like a giant steel and aluminum doughnut which rises 244 feet from ground level. As it climbs it rotates, making one and a half revolutions during the ascent. At the top of the tower the elevator continues revolving, making two com-

*On a clear day the Sky Tower at Marineland offers views
of Point Dume and Balboa*

plete circuits. Then, on the descent, it makes another one and a half trips around the spire. The whole operation takes four minutes and provides a panoramic view of all the Palos Verdes country as well as out to sea. In the wintertime it is an excellent spot to watch for migrating gray whales. Only from the Goodyear blimp could you have a rival view of the sea and seashore of southern California.

Marineland of the Pacific is located on Palos Verdes Drive West just as it becomes Palos Verdes Drive South. It is south of Palos Verdes Estates, Redondo, Hermosa and Manhattan, and northwest of San Pedro.

Rides on the Sky Tower are 50 cents for adults and 25 cents for children. Marineland and the Tower are open every day of the year from 10 a.m. until sunset.

From the Sky Tower seek out the haunt of Farouk, Woofy and Petula.

Storybook characters? Far from it. This trio is as real and substantial as any you'll ever meet. They are Arctic walruses and Marineland has had them since they were babies.

Collected by a Marineland expedition in April, 1961, they were taken near St. Lawrence Island in the Bering Straits. Two females were taken a few miles off the Siberian coast. Originally there were two pairs of walruses but one of the females, called Priscilla, died in 1968 of a stomach infection.

At the time each was a hundred-pound infant. They were flown from Alaska to Marineland and raised on a formula of pure whipping cream (sans sugar), minced clams, brewer's yeast and vitamins. One of the infants gained weight at a rate of one and three-quarter pounds a day. It wasn't until the walruses were two years old that they were weaned from the whipping cream diet. Since then they have subsisted on clams and bonito fillets.

The Vincent Thomas Bridge, opened in 1964, connects
Terminal Island with San Pedro

Today, Woofy, the jumbo of the lot, weighs 2,700 pounds and is about as sleek as a marble. The other two weigh nearly as much.

Experts at Marineland claim that the walruses actually perform for visitors, and especially well for small children. When I visited the park I expressed skepticism.

We stood and made faces through the heavy viewing glass at Woofy, not only the largest but the most gregarious of the lot. Woofy seemed to be performing. He pushed his blubbery, whiskery face against the glass and blew clouds of bubbles.

But just then a small girl appeared. Now there was no doubt. Woofy went into his please-the-small-children routine. First he rolled over on his back and blew a storm of bubbles. Then he swam down level with the little girl and banged his head against the glass. He clicked his teeth together loudly and to climax the display banged the window with one flipper.

It was hard to argue after such a show.

You can view the walruses from a platform topside where you can look down into the two pools—Farouk has one pool, Woofy and Petula the other—and see the walruses swimming or watch them clamber onto the concrete apron to sun or feed. Far better is the underwater viewing site where you can watch the great hulks swim effortlessly on their backs, kiss (they do a lot of this) and show off.

All of the animals grew tusks but two of them have had them removed. They enjoyed banging the concrete floor of the tanks with their tusks and there were dangers of abscesses. Woofy alone knew enough to favor his tusks and has been allowed to keep his.

There is no regular walrus show. It goes on all the time. When you explore this byway, bring a small child along, even if you have to borrow one. You'll get a better show at the underwater walrus view port that way.

One complaint: there should be benches at the underwater windows for those looking in at the walruses. A person can get tired standing for hours on end watching walrus shenanigans.

Almost as much fun to visit are the whales. But there is a difference. Farouk, Woofy and Petula seem to meet you more than halfway. The whales at Marineland are a little more reserved. Still they enjoy being scratched, babied, talked to.

While you'll enjoy the regular whale shows that are staged here (see them and the seal and dolphin shows by all means) it is interesting to study the whales, too, when they are not performing.

These are giant creatures, among the largest marine animals ever captured. On hand is Bubbles, a pilot whale, fifteen feet long and weighing 1,500 pounds. Bubbles has been trained to sing, dance, shake hands, wave good-bye, lift a barbell and leap completely out of the water.

And there is Swifty. Swifty is the first *Pseudorca crassidens*—false killer whale—captured alive. She comes equipped with a mouth filled with pointed teeth (Bubbles is more gently endowed). Swifty lets her trainer and good friends at Marineland put their hands in her mouth and she only pretends to nibble. She has been hand-fed since her first day of captivity. Today she is over fifteen feet long, weighs 1,500 pounds. She does an assortment of tricks, too. She'll jump twenty feet out of the water on command. Usually the spectators get splashed by this performance.

Both Bubbles and Swifty are perverse in this way. They seem to smile a fishy, deadpanned smile whenever their high jumps have dampened the audience.

Take time to look through the viewport at the whale tank at Bubbles and Swifty. If you are lucky, they might come over to the window and look back at you. They'll do it when their trainer is around.

A new addition to the whale family at Marineland is Orky, a killer whale, which has been taught to do a number of tricks. There

*The boat dock at Ports of Call, San Pedro, a collection of
some forty shops and restaurants*

is a new 1,300-seat stadium for Orky's show. Orky is more than fourteen feet long, weighs 3,000 pounds. In the tank with Orky are three common dolphins.

There are other smaller—but equally interesting—animals at Marineland. View the penguins, the lion-fish (with deadly spines), the giant sea bass (weighing 600 pounds), the great sea turtles (weighing 300 pounds) the moray eels and others.

From Marineland our course is along Palos Verdes Drive South to its junction with 25th Street in San Pedro. Then along that avenue to Gaffey, jog north to 22nd Street and continue east to Pacific Avenue.

South now, along Pacific Avenue, past Fort MacArthur, one of California's oldest military bases. This lower reservation was set aside by excutive order on September 14, 1888. The upper reservation, where coastal guns bristled until the end of World War II, was acquired in 1910. The guns are gone now, here instead is a small missile outpost. The post is named in honor of Lieutenant General Arthur MacArthur who died in 1912.

Past Fort MacArthur we come to a sign pointing down the hill to the east along Stephen M. White Drive to Cabrillo Beach, operated by the city of Los Angeles.

A great expanse of white sand invites bathers and sun-worshippers. A two-story marine museum is worth the visit, and there's a large parking lot where there is a parking fee in summer.

When the sea is calm, you can walk out on the mile-long breakwater; anglers are allowed to fish from it. But when the wind is kicking up white-caps in the bay and a sea is running, there is no admission to the breakwater and warning signs are posted. On such a day, a large wave could break clear across the narrow barrier and sweep anglers or sightseers into the water.

Offshore, whatever the wind, dozens of sailboats frolic, marking the gray water with their white sails.

142

The Princess, a small paddle-wheeler, makes short harbor cruises from Ports of Call

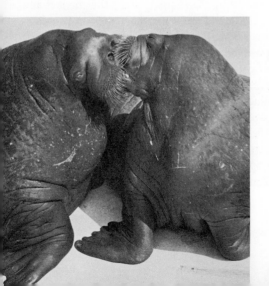

Woofy and Petula engage in kissing, a sport popular with these Marineland walruses

—Marineland

North again on Pacific Avenue to 22nd Street, east on this to
Crescent Avenue bending toward the northeast and along Crescent
Avenue to Harbor Boulevard. Enjoy here the salty sight of ships at
anchor, Navy vessels being loaded and outfitted. Close at hand is a
fueling station for Navy tankers. On Harbor Boulevard note the
many fishing boats tied up, nets out drying.

Near Twelfth Street is the parking area for one of the more colorful sites in San Pedro—Ports of Call.

Built in 1963, Ports of Call is a collection of some forty shops
and restaurants along the western edge of the main channel of Los
Angeles Harbor. Shake-roofed with shuttered windows and Dutch
doors, the buildings in the complex are a blend of English, Norman
and Mediterranean architecture. The cobblestone and brick walk-
ways are lined with gas lights.

You'll find Oriental curios, Mexican gifts, imports from Scandi-
navia here, and many others. A new addition is a Whaler's Village.

When Ports of Call was being built, the developers found an old
San Francisco ferryboat, the *Sierra Nevada,* in one of the ship
graveyards in the Bay area. She was overhauled, made seaworthy,
and towed south to Ports of Call. Now she houses shops, a snack
bar, benches to sit on to enjoy the shipping along the channel and
the sunshine.

A small paddle-wheeler, the *Princess,* offers short harbor
cruises. This double-decked vessel sails from Ports of Call every
hour on the hour on Friday evenings, Saturday and Saturday evenings, and on Sunday.

A Pierpoint Landing cruise boat also stops at Ports of Call to
pick up passengers for a more extensive cruise than a *Princess*
outing.

Not long ago you crossed the main channel between San Pedro
and Terminal Island by auto ferry. The ferry is gone (only a very
few remain in California) and in its place is the great gleaming

Vincent Thomas Bridge which opened in April, 1964. With a 1,500-foot center span and a total length of 6,060 feet, costing $21 million, the bridge was named after the assemblyman from the San Pedro district. Built by the state, it was turned over to the State Division of Bay Toll Crossings (which also operates the bridges at Dumbarton, San Mateo-Hayward, San Francisco-Oakland, Richmond-San Rafael, Carquinez, and Martinez).

The toll charge of 25 cents for the average passenger car is supposed to pay off the bridge cost in forty years.

Here our byways ends. You are bound to find more to explore: some people pass Saturdays and Sundays exploring the docks, visiting Navy vessels on display, visiting Pierpoint Landing.

Take one of the harbor cruises if you have never done so. Meet the tough little tugs and fireboats, watch the auto freighters unload and the loading of metal scrap.

The harbor has a come-again effect on most people. And certainly once you meet Woofy at Marineland, you will come this way again, if, for no other reason, than to watch him put on his 2,700-pound act.

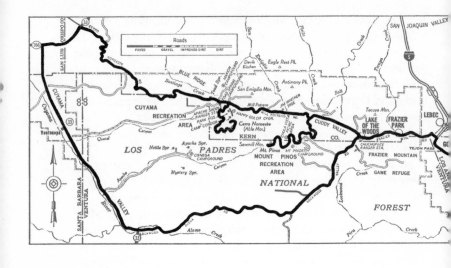

XIII AROUND THE SOUTHERN PEAKS OF KERN COUNTY

Fun to explore—be careful in deep winter
Length of exploration—can be driven in a day

THE BEST ROADS to explore are the least-traveled ones, and surely there are few avenues in Kern County that know less traffic by late springtime than those that probe and circle Mount Pinos, Sawmill Mountain and Abel Mountain.

These prominences sit right on Kern County's southern edge and some of the access roads reach over into adjoining Ventura County.

By spring this is green-up country. Provide a winter with respectable rainfall and some snow, and there will be a profusion of wild flowers. There will be running water in the springs and streams to keep the *potreros* lush with grass. The conifers that stand on the sides of the tall mountains will be healthy and ripe with perfume. It can be a smiling land. Exploring by summer and fall is invited. Only by stormy winter, when snow visits some of the higher elevations, and when some of the dirt roads could be muddy and bogged, should you avoid the more rural areas.

If this bulk of mountains has a name, the geographers have been reluctant to advertise the fact. Call them an extension of the Tehachapis if you will. Many people do, and few argue. Some claim them to be merely an eastern bulking of the Coast Range. But here, in the Los Padres National Forest, it seems that geographers are content to let the mountain mass go unnamed, except for the prominences. There are a series of 8,000-foot peaks in the region. Far to the south are the Topatopas, and to the east, on the

147

A dirt road leads to the summit of Mount Pinos where gnarled Jeffrey pines present unusual silhouettes. Some small specimens of the rarer limber pine also grow nearby

other side of the Ridge Route, are the Tehachapis proper. But the links are semantic—it is all contiguous mountain country.

For all its empty byways, the region has known people for more than a hundred years. There were Indians here in the old days and they fashioned such wonders as the extravagantly painted cave in the remote Pleito country. Coastal Indians, fleeing from the mission fathers in Santa Barbara, are said to have fled into the San Emigdio country here after an uprising.

There are old borax, antimony and gold mines. Early-day sawmills dotted this passage and bears were known in the region. The Mill Potrero Road, still an unspoiled, unpaved track, was once known as the Camino Viejo—the old road—and it was supposed to have been the earliest wagon route by which the settlers in the Frazier Park-Cuddy Valley area could travel to the San Joaquin Valley.

There are roads here, wide paved highways, jeep courses, and trails. There are strange sights such as the Devil's Kitchen. There are record trees and pleasant fields of Jeffrey pines on the high mesas, where the ground is littered with cones and pine needles and the gray squirrels forage. There are pinyon pines, and nut hunters—bird, animal and human—make a pilgrimage here by fall. There are campgrounds that say "stay awhile" and magic, sweet mountain water.

The best way to get to the approaches of this fair country from the south is via the Ridge Route—U.S. Highway 99. This historic avenue is undergoing many changes in its transformation into an all eight-lane freeway thoroughfare. Old landmarks will change and disappear. For this trip travel north of Gorman to the Frazier Mountain side road leading to the west. Take this avenue through the two communities of Frazier Park and Lake of the Woods. On the edge of the latter town there is a road fork. The left hand branch leads back to the local district ranger station at Chuchu-

149

pate, to Lockwood Valley and to State Highway 33 some twenty-seven miles distant. This will be our return route on a loop trip.

We take the right hand road at the fork, the one signed "To Mt. Pinos." A slight hill is climbed and then picturesque Cuddy Valley is gained, the area first settled in this region.

About four miles along this course is a side road on the right, a dirt track, with a Forest Service sign directing the traveler to the Tecuya country. The Tecuya region is that last big ridge of mountains that separates, the Cuddy Valley from the San Joaquin Valley. Most of these mountain avenues are jeep roads, and are so designated. The roads are steep, narrow and primitive, and more than one conventional automobile has gotten into trouble here. But for four-wheel-drive vehicles they are a joy. Further along our route, the Cuddy Valley Road, another side road reveals the wonders of Pleito Canyon. Antimony Peak and Eagle Rest Peak are close at hand. And the horrendous Devil's Kitchen, a fiery cauldron of stone by summer, beckons.

A short distance beyond this turnoff, still traveling on the Cuddy Valley highway, the road bends to the left and we come to the turn-off of the Mill Potrero Road, a nine-mile unpaved course along the north side of Mount Pinos and Abel Mountain.

It is a good idea to check at the Chuchupate Ranger Station to determine the condition of this unpaved byway. Often it is rutted and rough after a winter's rains. The Forest Service usually gives it a single blading in the spring—that has to last all year as a rule.

The name "Mill Potrero Road" most likely comes from the old antimony mill that lies hidden in the rubble in the bottom of the canyon there. It dates back to the last century. Old sawmills once stood in the canyon country, too, giving the region a double reason for its place name.

A *potrero* is a grassy area, a pasture ground. Part way along the

150

—*Union Pacific*

Along a winding road between Abel Mountain and High-
way 33, poppies, lupine and fiddleneck bloom in profusion

passage of this road such an area stands, a great meadowland where cattle graze.

Here stands the record Jim Whitener Tree, a ponderosa pine discovered in 1942 by Forest Service ranger Whitener. It is twenty-one feet in circumference, 142 feet tall, has a spread of sixty-five feet, truly a forest giant. It sits in the bottom of a canyon, so much of its bulk is not instantly apparent. But when one stands beside the bole it is a different story.

A record big-cone spruce, believed to be the largest in the world, is hidden in nearby Pleito Canyon.

To the north now raises San Emigdio Mountain, this peak 7,495 feet high.

The Mill Potrero Park private camp is passed. Jeffrey pines abound in the area. Then the road begins to climb and at Apache Saddle it gains pavement again. Nearby is the Apache Saddle Ranger Station of the Forest Service.

The course now is to the left, to the south. A short distance away is the outpost of the Kern County Recreation Department and the facilities of Happy Gulch camping area and Condor Camp, a facility of the Westside Children's Camp Association.

Up the northeast side of Abel Mountain toward the summit the road is paved, with a gradual climb and few sharp turns.

By season this is a popular winter sports area, for snow sits heavily on Abel Mountain (otherwise known as Cerro Noroeste). Its summit is 8,286 feet and even in late spring there can be patches of snow on the ground in the deep shade.

Near the summit is the ski tow and the ski hut of Camp Alto. Beyond is the Campo Alto Campground, under a great canopy of shade offered by aged conifers, with spots for trailers and campers. The bulk of the summit here is flat and invites casual exploration. There are some excellent overlooks to the west, out over the pale scar left by the Cuyama River. The Sierra Madre Ridge hides in the haze in the distance. To the south can be seen the treed uplift of Sawmill Mountain, the second tallest of the three peaks we'll explore: 8,800 feet.

Back down the Abel Mountain road now, we return to Apache Saddle and head toward the northwest. We come to the turnoff to the left onto the dirt road that follows down Quatal Canyon. Toad Springs Forest Service campground lies off on this side road. To the right is a spur road—also unpaved—that leads back to the small Marion Campground.

A shoulder of hills called Blue Ridge breaks the horizon to the north. This is largely cattle graze here, fenced fields that have been invaded by spring by a dozen kinds of wildflowers. The poppy expanses are the most impressive of any in Kern County, some of them ten acres in size, clump upon clump of the golden flowers, blooming for weeks in late spring. There are lupine here, coreopsis and a score of other brilliant blooms.

At the junction with State Highway 33 we head south, past the highway turnoff west into New Cuyama via State route 166, along the edge of the green fields and then the sandy wash of the Cuyama River.

The tiny community of Ventucopa is passed—the outpost's name a marriage of Ventura and Maricopa. To the left is the road leading into Quatal Canyon—rough and dusty.

Farther south we come to another dirt road leading eastward; this one, likewise rough and dusty, leads back into Apache Canyon and the Nettle Spring and Cienega Campgrounds. Mystery Spring and Apache Spring hide back along this bumpy course.

It is twenty-three miles from the entrance onto the Lockwood Valley Road to where we will leave it. The sign here will point toward the east and will advertise the route to Lockwood Valley and Frazier Park. The Chuchupate Ranger station is twenty-seven miles away.

*The Mill Potrero Road, an unpaved track, runs
along a canyon bottom on the north side of
Mount Pinos and Abel Mountain*

Again, we have a paved road the entire distance. Some of it is twisted and pregnant with hills, but it can be maneuvered without difficulty. It crosses a couple of streams, climbs some strange rock formations and runs through some pleasant flatland. Always to the north is the swell of Abel Mountain, Sawmill Mountain and finally, Mount Pinos.

Back at the original Lake of the Woods fork we take the same road up the hill into Cuddy Valley. This time we drive on past the Mill Potrero Road and climb toward the summit of Mount Pinos.

This is another mountain that knows winter sports in the snow season. By spring its trails are happy magnets. You'll find a fine one along the highway—the McGill Trail that leads three and one half miles up from the road to the McGill Campground higher on Mount Pinos. There is a parking area at the bottom of it.

The Mount Pinos and Chula Vista campgrounds are passed as the road approaches the summit. At the end of the pavement there is a large paved area, designed mainly for the winter sports parking, and a small picnic site, which is going to be phased out by the Forest Service. A dirt road leading uphill takes the explorer higher into the Jeffrey and ponderosa and white fir forests to the summit of Mount Pinos—8,831 feet—and through some uncommon stands of limber pine. There is exotic ming moss here, too, at the top elevations.

At the peak of Mount Pinos is a radio relay station which connects Edwards Air Force Base with Vandenberg Air Force Base. There are some great gnarly old Jeffrey pines near the summit, wind-tortured trees that present unusual silhouettes.

The summit of Mount Pinos is a good vantage point from which to look for condors. The big birds, which roost in the Sespe country and bathe in the Sisquoc preserve, frequently fly over Mount Pinos on their long-range scavenger flights. They usually travel in pairs, ride the thermals without flapping their wings, are greatly

155

curious. They find frequent deer carcasses in season on the slopes of Mount Pinos.

The old sawmills in the country are gone now. Only the most knowledgeable old-timers can hike into the Mill Potrero country to the crumbling site of the ancient antimony mill. The borax mine is abandoned. And gold is no longer placered from the sites of Mount Pinos.

But still the charm about the country remains—it is in the trees, the black oaks and the pinyon; it is in the wild flowers out by Toad Springs, and the yucca that burns so brightly in bloom.

From the high places there is quiet and much to see. The joy here is in the small crowds and the far horizons.

XIV AROUND NEWPORT BAY COUNTRY

Fun to explore—anytime of the year
Length of exploration—can be driven in a day

"IT HAS ALL CHANGED SO," said an old-timer, looking from the headland out over the peninsula of Newport and Balboa and at the slender bay there.

"There was a time when sailing ships came up the harbor and unloaded lumber here. That's how the McFaddens got their start. In lumber."

Below, on the Pacific Coast Highway, traffic poured along unmindful of the history. Concrete and glass apartment houses crowded in on the bay. Offshore was the opulence of Lido Isle and beyond the beach houses of Balboa ran south along the edge of the ocean.

Newport got its name in the beginning because it was just that—a new port between San Diego and San Pedro. And business in 1863 was good. When Captain S. S. Dunnels gingerly pushed the *Vaquero,* a low freeboard side-wheeler, through the mouth of the Santa Ana River into the harbor, past the mud flats, unloaded lumber from San Diego and picked up a cargo of hides and produce from the green fields above the sandstone bluffs, he knew he had found a good thing.

Dunnels and D. M. Dormann fashioned a stubby dock here on the mainland side of the estuary and continued to conduct business. In time the area became known as Newport Landing.

In 1873 James and Robert McFadden bought the *Vaquero* and the landing from Dunnels and Dormann. Business continued

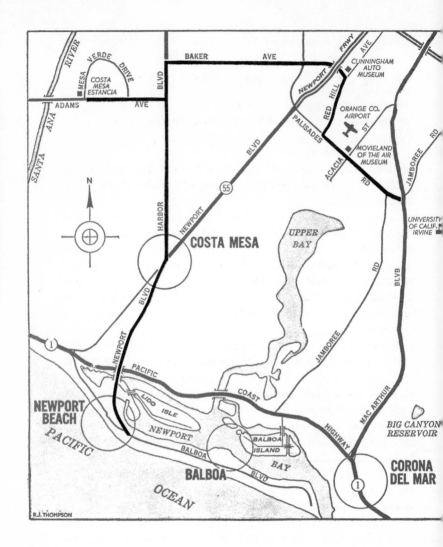

158

briskly. By 1876 they were able to contract for a new steamer, one to be built in San Francisco and to be called the *Newport*.

In 1878 there was a change at Newport Landing. The McFaddens sold out to the Pacific Coast Steamship Co. and became agents for that firm.

Ten years later they formed the Newport Wharf and Lumber Co., and on the ocean side started work on the first municipal pier at Newport.

They formed the Santa Ana and Newport Railroad, bought rails, smoothed out a roadbed and put down the steel. By 1889 the McFaddens were buying swampland and mudflats in the harbor area—nearly 1,000 acres—for $1.00 an acre from the government. The mud flats were not part of the ranch lands.

The steel rails connected with the Santa Fe at Santa Ana, and on January 12, 1891, the first train made the run.

With a train offering an easy route from Santa Ana instead of the rutted and chuck-holed wagon road, campers flocked to the beach by summer. Emil Brockett built a store near the end of the track and in the store, on August 11, 1891, the first Newport post office opened.

The following year the enterprising McFaddens laid out the townsite of Newport and 550 ships unloaded at their pier. The railroad sent a spur north to Shell Beach (it would later be called Huntington Beach) so they could haul celery to Newport.

But the size of the business now dismayed the McFaddens. They sought to sell the operation to someone, someone small, not one of the large railroads. After the transaction had been consummated they discovered that the new owner was the Southern Pacific Railroad. They claimed they had been tricked and in disgust started selling their land holdings in the Newport area.

The Southern Pacific was not interested in Newport as a port,

Concrete and glass apartment buildings crowd in on New-
port Bay, and the sides of the harbor are lined with
pleasure craft of every size and description

and they did not care to see the short line railroad flourish. The Newport and Santa Ana Railroad fell on unhappy days.

The land was cut up in parcels and offered for sale. Newport Beach was the name of the new site. Henry Huntington invested in the property in 1904 and later would run the big red cars down from Los Angeles and Long Beach through Huntington Beach and along the peninsula to Balboa.

Real estate boomed and the land filled up. Lido Island was fashioned out of mud flats and dredgings. The port city idea was gone now. Newport Beach would be a community of gracious living. Newport incorporated in 1906 and growth has marked each year since.

"It has all changed so," the old-timer remarked as he looked out over the apartment houses, the swank shopping center, the broad avenues and fine houses.

"In the old days side-wheelers poked into the harbor."

Boats still use the harbor. Hundreds of them. The sides of the harbor are lined with pleasure craft of every description. Colored sails flap here in the working winds and great cabin cruisers parade, haughty and quiet, down through the harbor and out to catch the moving sea.

This byway is a quest to find something of the days of the *Vaquero* and the McFaddens. It is a difficult chore, this seeking of yesterday, but happily there are a few landmarks.

Start then at Newport Beach and drive north on Newport Boulevard, then north along Harbor Boulevard to Adams Avenue and west to Mesa Verde Drive West. Here, saved for seekers of yesterday, is the Costa Mesa *estancia,* a rare bird in a changing world.

A minor mystery concerns the *estancia*. Built during mission days—some think around 1817 or a year or two later—the outpost occupied lonely ground.

If it was built as a way station for travelers from San Juan Capis-

—*Title Insurance & Trust Company*

*By 1908 or 1909, when this photograph was taken, the idea of a
port city was gone. Newport Beach would be, instead,
a community of gracious living*

*The Costa Mesa estancia stands on old Indian grounds. Excava-
tions have uncovered several Indian burials and have revealed
bits of broken shell, the typical midden of an Indian site*

trano to San Gabriel, why was it located ten miles off the line of march along El Camino Real? Or, if it was an outpost to shelter *vaqueros* from San Juan Capistrano, why were the grazing fields so far from the home mission?

Two separate archaeological excavations have revealed that the *estancia* was built on old Indian grounds. This is evident even today, for the darkened soil around the building is shot through with bits of broken shell, the typical midden of an old Indian site.

In addition, the WPA-sponsored Adams-Fairview excavation in 1935 uncovered several Indian burials. Some were in good condition, some had been disturbed by vandals and animals, others had almost vanished because of age.

The Pacific Coast Archaeological Society excavations in 1965 were labeled disappointing. No burials nor old material, either Indian or of the Mission period, were unearthed.

Following the Mission period the *estancia* became the home of Don Diego Sepulveda and appears thus on period maps. Later still it became part of a ranch house, then was owned for seventeen years by an historic character of the area, Gabe Allen, and eventually it passed to the Adams family for whom the nearby road is named. In 1939 it was known as the Derby Ranch.

In 1940 the property was purchased by the Segerstrom family of Costa Mesa and in 1963 the *estancia* and a five-acre plot of ground were deeded to the city of Costa Mesa as a memorial to the early settlers of the area.

The building was renovated. The frame covering was removed, the adobe walls strengthened and realigned. A roof that would protect the early construction was built and today the Costa Mesa *estancia* is California Historical Landmark Number 227. It is lovingly tended by the Costa Mesa Historical Society. The three rooms of the building have been outfitted—one as a Mission-period kitchen, one as a Spanish-American period living room, one as a Victorian-period bedroom and study.

The grounds are well cared for, and ancient pepper trees still shade the area.

The landmarks we seek here take various forms. One is old automobiles. Return along Adams Avenue to Harbor Boulevard and north on that divided road to Baker Avenue. Then east, under the Newport Freeway to Red Hill Avenue.

People of Costa Mesa are accustomed to seeing antique cars on their streets. Gleaming Rolls Royces and Dusenbergs and Packards get little more than an indulgent smile these days. Residents know that the cars come from the vast Briggs Cunningham Automotive Museum—at the corner of Baker Avenue and Red Hill Avenue—and that they are being driven because it is considered by the operators of the Museum to be the best kind of medicine for antique cars.

Cunningham, millionaire sportsman, has assembled at the Museum a collection of classic cars that marks the significant points of the evolution of the automobile. Here is a 1912 Rauch and Lang electric, a battery-powered beauty that runs whisper-quiet and attracts more than casual attention wherever it goes. The electric car, the experts declare, is the car of the future; and while the Rauch and Lang, fifty-five years old, is no freeway competitor, still it is an interesting possibility in solving the problems of modern transportation.

Visit the 1927 Bugatti Royale. One of the most expensive cars ever built, it was specifically designed for royalty. Some put today's value of the enormous sedan at $75,000. Cunningham's staff has it in pristine condition.

Study the American Underslung made in 1911 with its forty-one inch wheels.

Admire that 1935 Dusenberg sports roadster once owned by

164

The Spad (background) and
the Pfalz are two of the World
War I planes on display at
the Movieland of the Air
museum. There are planes of
World War II vintage as well

—MGA Enterprises

This 1914 Mercedes, on display at the Briggs Cunningham Automotive Museum, was a member of the famous "White Team"
that won the French Grand Prix just weeks before
World War I

—Strother Macminn

Gary Cooper. Ask the attendants at the Museum to start up the motor. It purrs.

Here is the famed 1928 Hispano-Suiza roadster, a 1914 Mercedes, the beloved Mercer Raceabout of 1912, a 1915 Pierce Arrow, a 1923 Stutz Super Bear Cat.

The display is endless, and fascinating. Each car is marked with a large descriptive placard. But better, make the tour of the Museum with one of the experts here. Major-domo John Burgess, himself an automobile racer, technician and artist, is happiest when he is relating anecdotes about each car.

Burgess will spend extra time telling you about the cars Cunningham built or designed. Here, for example, is the slabsided "Le Monstre" Cunningham, that the Museum's owner raced at Le Mans in 1950. There are other Le Mans cars here built and raced by Cunningham.

Many of the automobiles on display have racing backgrounds. Such is the Birdcage Maserati, so called because of the intricate tubular construction of the prize-winning Le Mans entry.

Here is a 1913 Peugeot that raced in the Grand Prix circuit, a 1919 Ballot of Indianapolis racetrack fame, a 1942 Ferrari with a racing body.

At last count more than sixty-five landmark cars were in the Briggs Cunningham collection. Others, such as a pair of dragsters, are displayed on loan. On the immaculate work benches in the rear of the Museum technicians are restoring a vintage Bugatti.

Cunningham's wish is to present to the public a working museum of vintage cars. The personnel can cite chapter and verse of automotive history, and often show old racing films.

Beyond the Automotive Museum is the Movieland of the Air museum, located off Palisades Road on Acacia Street. Here, in a large hangar and parked on the edge of the Orange County Airport, are dozens of historic planes. Here are the adversaries of

World War I: the Sopwith Camel, the Spad, the Nieuport—and the Fokker and the Pfalz. Some of the old planes were auctioned off in 1968.

Here, too, are the planes that fought in World War II: the Corsair, the Mustang, the Hellcat. In the adjacent International Flight and Space Museum is a field filled with jet planes and missiles.

Southeast on Palisades Road leads the explorer to MacArthur Boulevard. Off in the distance can be seen the modern structures of the University of California at Irvine.

This is all Irvine Ranch Country, this rural area behind Costa Mesa, Newport Beach, Balboa and Corona del Mar. Jackrabbits still play in the fields and hawks hunt overhead. Yet only minutes away are the concrete and glass apartments and shopping centers of the beach cities.

Yeterday, disguised variously, *can* be found in this country, but the joys of the side-wheeler *Vaquero,* the old Newport and the Santa Ana Railroad are past. The mud flats in the estuary have been filled and planted with homes. Even the Santa Ana River has been channeled so that it no longer deposits silt from the distant San Bernardino Mountains in the bay.

Still, by walking out to the end of the municipal pier at Newport Beach, it is possible to picture the steamer *Newport* putting in with a load of lumber at McFadden wharf. A visit to the old *estancia,* under the shade of the old pepper trees, is enough to put the legendary chest-high mustard back in the fields and bring visitors on horseback to taste the outpost's hospitality.

The ancient Rauch and Lang and Stutz and Sopwith Camel speak their own language of yesterday, pleasant to savor.

Orange County, more than any in the state, has pictured change and modernization. Happily these landmarks of yesterday are still there.

167

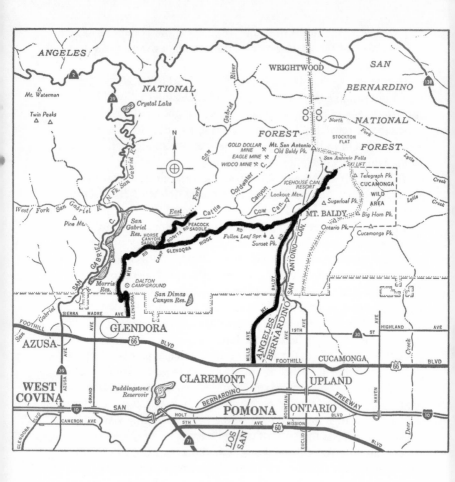

XV INTO THE COLORFUL MOUNT BALDY COUNTRY

Fun to visit—sometimes closed in deep winter
Length of exploration—can all be seen in a day

A FOREST SERVICE LOOKOUT sighted the strange creature on the ground near the vantage point late one afternoon. He saw it from his station at the Sunset Peak tower in the Angeles National Forest north of Claremont.

It was a bird of some sort, but it was big, bigger than a jay or a crow, bigger than a pheasant.

It was walking slowly, head down, feeding like a barnyard animal.

"What would a turkey be doing in this country?" radioed the puzzled lookout to the Forest Service dispatcher.

There was a long moment while memories were searched. Then someone remembered. Wild turkeys had been planted by the California Fish and Game Department in the Mount Baldy area in the 1930s. The plant never took. The birds released in Prairie Fork and Coldwater Canyon and Brown's Flat had never been seen again.

But here was a lone, wild, hen turkey not more than two miles from Baldy Village.

The wild turkey is only one of the strange sights that people have seen in the Baldy country, a region that supports the San Gabriel Mountains' highest peak and most scenic byway, old gold and copper mines, exotic animal life, a history of classic proportions and scenery to rival anything this side of the Sierras.

Old Baldy's vital statistics are as follows: its more formal name

169

is Mount San Antonio and its elevation is 10,064 feet. From its summit you can see for days deep into southern California. On a hazeless day you can see the southern Sierra Nevada's knife-ridge of peaks glistening in the morning sun.

Mount San Antonio smiles down on a network of fine, high trails rimming the Baldy bowl which are walked more each year. Each weekend from June, when the last of the old snow has melted and ice is gone from the footpaths, until around Thanskgiving, when the first new snow flies, the trails around Kelly's Camp, Thunder Mountain and West Baldy know the beat of hobnail soles.

The roads that provide easy access to the Baldy country are pleasure-driving joys. The slower avenue, the Glendora Mountain road, begins at the northern edge of Glendora, then switchbacks and meanders uphill and along rim-tops back to Baldy Village.

San Antonio Canyon supports a pair of roads. The older, lower road, dates back to 1893, when the first wagon course was whittled from the narrow canyon and the blocking hogbacks. A monumental right-of-way battle between Charles N. Baynham and the San Antonio Water Company followed, but Baynham was finally won over by the water company and the old toll road was established. For years vintage automobiles made the rugged trip over the toll road, until 1922 when the two counties—Los Angeles and San Bernardino—bought the route and converted it into a public thoroughfare.

The new, high road, built in 1955, does not have the steep pitches still found on the older, lower road.

San Antonio Canyon has known many tribulations. There have been tragic hiking accidents. Avalanches have caused fatalities at Movie Slope. In the big flood of 1938 hundreds of cabins in the village were washed away. Fire has threatened the canyon more than once. On Sunday afternoons in August the roads into the

170

Sturdy flatlanders can hike the Devil's Backbone between Baldy Notch and the summit of Old Baldy

Village are jammed with traffic, and surprise snowstorms in January can pin down for hours Village visitors who are without chains.

But by late fall the air is winy, the old-timers have more time to talk about the yesterdays of gold mining and the toll road, and a ride up the chair lift seems the most exciting jaunt in the world.

We start our byway exploration at Sierra Madre Avenue and the Glendora Mountain Road in northern Glendora. Follow the latter avenue past the Dalton percolation basin and the Little Dalton Forest Service Campground. Now the byway bends back toward the south and goes to work in its zigzag fashion to gain altitude. Soon you will be able to stop at a turnout and peer deep down into the San Gabriel Valley.

In time the zigzagging ceases and the road follows a northerly direction, still climbing gradually. At the road fork at Horse Canyon Saddle the Camp Bonita portion of the avenue is gained and the byway drops down to the East Fork of the San Gabriel River and the site of the vanished 1860s camp of Eldoradoville.

This tent and shack city spread for more than two miles along the turbulent East Fork, and from their crude habitations here the miners claimed fine placer gold from the gravels.

The San Gabriel River's Mother Lode was never discovered, although hard-rock mines have dotted the higher peaks to the north and east, toward the headwaters of the river.

Eldoradoville enjoyed a brief notoriety and was then washed away by the flood of 1862. Nothing of the old camp remains. Not one photograph of the colorful old gold camp, which was in existence for at least three years, has ever been found. Canyon historian Sedley Peck relates: "It boasted three general stores, and a half dozen saloons with their gambling and dance halls running wide open. John Robb, who spent more than sixty years of his life in the canyon, claimed that he made more money by running sawdust from the Union Saloon through his sluice box than he was able to

172

make from real mining, so prodigal and careless of their pokes were the miners and the gamblers of those days."

Weekend miners still try their hand at panning for placer gold in the East Fork near the junction of the Glendora Mountain Road.

Back at Horse Canyon Saddle it is the Gendora Ridge Road that runs on through the high country toward Baldy Village.

From this byway there are vistas to the east, into the Tanbark Flats area, the burned out Experimental Forest—a victim of the 1962 Johnston fire.

Great treeless Baldy stands to the north, its south face a chute that feeds into Cattle Canyon. In time Coldwater and Cow Canyon drainages will be seen.

At an unsigned spot along the road is historic Peacock Saddle. "People stole the signs for the spot as fast as we put them up, so we finally stopped putting them up," a ranger on the Baldy district explained.

Here the road cuts through the old Peacock Copper Mine, an ore producer of the 1920s. A search of the area by a canny rock-hound may disclose the small lode of azurite and malachite that is said to exist in the area.

This byway is a great favorite of sports car drivers. It is narrow, full of curves and varies little here in elevation. But the price the careless pay is high. Each year a half dozen or more of the small cars go off the edge here, and it is a tremendous drop-off. Cars are never brought up from the thousand-foot drop; they are stripped and left in the gorge. Forest Service people view the road with enormous mistrust. In bad weather when they have business in the East Fork, they usually drive down the San Antonio Canyon Road, across on Foothill, and back up into the San Gabriel River country on Highway 39, rather than chance a mishap. But on clear days the drive is a scenic delight; motorists who take their time and use

173

the turnouts for sight-seeing will have a rewarding time on the Glendora Mountain Road and the Glendora Ridge Road.

Near the end of the Ridge Road there are two watering places. Here is Fallen Leaf Spring, in a shady copse of evergreens, and a little farther along, Forked Spruce Spring.

Beyond, the road comes to Cow Canyon Saddle. From here an eleven-mile truck trail reaches back into the Coldwater Canyon area. The scar of the road tracing down the far side of Cow Canyon can be seen for miles from the Glendora Ridge Road. This truck trail crosses private property in the interior and so is gated. (It ends at an old Forest Service campground.) From here it is a number of miles, via unmaintained trails, to the Widco, Eagle and Gold Dollar gold mines. These have been inactive for at least twenty years.

Bighorn sheep have been spotted on at least one occasion on the Glendora Ridge Road. They range through all the high country of the south face of Baldy and beyond. Near the historical Widman Ranch in Coldwater Canyon black bear, bobcats, deer, coyotes, even a furtive mountain lion have been sighted.

The Glendora Ridge Road at last makes a downward pitch, runs through Yucca Flat (an area that knows a bumper crop of yucca blossoms every spring), and meets the Mount Baldy Road just below the Village.

It is a community of 500. There are more than 300 cabins, a grade school with 100 children, a fire station, a ranger station (the Forest Service adminsters the area) and typical resort businesses.

The Mount Baldy Trout Farm is open throughout the year.

Here is the Icehouse Canyon resort. Additional parking is available here for hikers using the Icehouse Canyon trail up to Icehouse Saddle and beyond to Kelly's Camp, to the Cucamonga Wilderness, to Cucamonga Peak and Ontario Peak. Off to the north from

*In 1908 this touring group paid 75 cents to use the
San Antonio Canyon toll road*

Icehouse Saddle are the prominences of Telegraph Peak and Thunder Mountain, on a course that runs on to Baldy Notch.

Beyond Icehouse, on the Mount Baldy Road now, is the non-charge Forest Service campground of Glacier, the improved, charge campground at Manker. A side road bends away to the west and runs back to San Antonio Falls, noisy by spring.

Then Movie Slope and the 1,000-car parking area for the Mount Baldy Ski Lift.

Here is one of the scenic joys of the Canyon. The double chair lift follows a 4,100-foot course and lifts from 6,500 feet at the parking area to 7,800 feet at Baldy Notch. The lift is accompanied part of the way by a noisy stream. Stellar jays often flit over the towers ahead of the traveler and call from the white firs that grow along the slope.

At Baldy Notch there is an assortment of pleasures. If early snow has fallen, there are two more chair lifts on which to plumb the skiing area. If it is still summery there is dry-land skiing (on straw), with lessons for youngsters and less agile devotees. Until the snow flies you'll find musicians and dancers on hand to entertain.

For the sturdiest visitors there is the two-mile road that climbs stiffly toward the Devil's Backbone. Once on this narrow spine of mountains, it is two more miles out to the summit of Old Baldy. From here the exhausted flatlander will probably retreat to the swift descent of the chair lift. Others of sterner stuff may want to hike on for eleven miles back to Baldy Village by the way of West Baldy and Bear Canyon.

By summer Herb Leffler, founder and operator of the Baldy Ski Lifts, books running races up the Forest Service truck trail that leads for four miles from San Antonio Falls to the Notch. Leather-lunged runners have been known to extend the race all the way to Baldy's summit.

There is another truck trail, gated to automobiles, that leads down the back side of the Notch into the Stockton Flat region of Lytle Creek. It is a steep course.

Both San Antonio Canyon and Lytle Creek knew gold mining in the early days: The Lytle placers came first, then the hardrock Banks Mine in San Antonio Canyon. The Banks property later was known as the Hocumac, after the first letters of the names of three early-day miners: Holcomb, Cushion and MacKay.

In addition to gold the canyon has offered up graphite and even lapis lazuli, the latter on an active claim in Cascade Canyon, a tributary to San Antonio.

To complete the byway exploration loop we follow the Mount Baldy Road south, past Movie Slope—a ski area by winter—Manker, Glacier, Icehouse, the Village, down the hill on the new, high road in San Antonio Canyon through a pair of tunnels to the valley.

The route is swift and easy. The road is wide and there are frequent turnouts for those who would pause and look over the ridge to the east, down to the older road that followed the stream.

From the start of the Glendora Mountain Road, up along the knife-edge route of the Glendora Ridge Road, to Baldy Village and on up San Antonio Canyon to the Notch—this is country of exceptional scenic values. The uplifted mountain faces are enormous. Good hiking trails beckon the walker and pleasant campsites lure the stay-awhile people.

"I've lived in the Canyon since 1921," one inhabitant related. "I've yet to remember a day in it that I didn't like." Those years covered several vigorous winters, but San Antonio Canyon has that appeal. No visitor will come away unrewarded.

BIBLIOGRAPHY

California, A Guide to the Golden State, American Guide Series. New York, N. Y. Hastings House, 1954.

Crowe, Earle. *Men of El Tejon.* Los Angeles, Calif. The Ward Ritchie Press, 1957.

Cullimore, Clarence. *Old Adobes of Forgotten Fort Tejon.* Bakersfield, Calif. Kern County Historical Society, 1941.

Fowler, Harlan D. *Camels to California.* Stanford, Calif. Stanford University Press, 1950.

Gudde, Erwin G. *California Place Names.* Berkeley, Calif. University of California Press, 1960.

Hanna, Phil Townsend. *The Dictionary of California Land Names.* Los Angeles, Calif. Automobile Club of Southern Calif., 1946.

Kroeber, A. L. *Handbook of the Indians of California.* Berkeley, Calif. California Book Co., Ltd., 1953.

Layne, J. Gregg. *Western Wayfaring.* Los Angeles, Calif. Automobile Club of Southern California, 1954.

Leadabrand, Russ. *A Guidebook to the San Gabriel Mountains.* The Ward Ritchie Press, 1967.

————. *A Guidebook to the Mojave Desert.* Los Angeles, Calif. The Ward Ritchie Press, 1966.

Outland, Charles. *Man-Made Disaster.* Glendale, Calif. The Arthur H. Clark Co., 1963.

Robinson, W. W. *The Story of the Southwest Museum.* Los Angeles, Calif. The Ward Ritchie Press, 1960.

Saunders, Charles Francis. *The Southern Sierras of California.* New York, N. Y. Houghton Mifflin Co., 1923.

Trails Magazine, twenty issues, quarterly, 1934 to 1939, edited by Will H. Thrall; two issues, E. C. Bower, acting editor.

Vernon, Charles Clark. *A History of the San Gabriel Mountains.* Los Angeles, Calif. The Historical Society of Southern California Quarterly, four issues, March, June, September, December, 1956.

INDEX

180

181